STEP BY STEP
영작문

HU::iNE

STEP BY STEP
영작문

성 은 경

머리말

영어로 의사소통을 제대로 하기 위해서는 말하기, 듣기, 읽기뿐만 아니라, 쓰기 능력까지 골고루 갖추어야 한다. 그러나 영어를 오랫동안 공부한 사람조차도 작문에는 자신 없어한다. 이 책은 실제 생활에서 자주 사용되는 표현을 중심으로, 초보자도 쉽고 재미있게 영작문에 다가갈 수 있도록 하는데 주안점을 두었다.

이 책에서는 단락(paragraph), 브레인스토밍(brainstorming), 개요(outlining)의 개념에서부터 출발하여 다양한 형태의 글쓰기를 단계적으로 소개하고 있다. 각 unit마다 실생활에서 흔히 접하게 되는 회화를 통해서 영어식 표현을 배우는 Our Life, 한국 대학생들이 쓴 글을 영어 원어민 선생님이 직접 수정해 주는 과정을 보여주는 Writing Process, 기본적인 문장 구조와 다양한 문장 형태를 보여주는 Sentence Structure, 영작문에 필요한 문법을 소개하는 Grammar 부분 등이 나온다. 나아가 여러 가지 Task를 통하여 학습자들이 배운 내용을 응용하여 실제로 작문을 연습할 수 있도록 하였다.

영작문은 Native Speaker들도 가장 어려워하는 분야이다. 그러나 외국어로서 영어를 배우는 우리 입장에서 보면, 영작문은 Native Speaker들과의 격차를 가장 쉽게 줄일 수 있는 영역이기도 하다. 모쪼록 이 책이 영작문을 Step by Step으로 익히는데 도움이 되기를 바란다.

2013년 3월

저자 성은경

차 례

Unit 1

Introducing Ourselves and Others I

INTRODUCTION

Topic: Introducing ourselves and others
Writing Process: Paragraph form, brainstorming and outlining
Grammar: Sentences and fragments

주제: 우리들과 다른 사람들을 소개하기
글쓰기: 단락 형태, 브레인 스토밍과 개요 작성
문법: 문장과 문장의 일부

OUR LIFE

Setting: the welcome lounge of Super Duper English Academy
Characters: Katherine, head of native English teachers at the academy; and mischievous Fred, a newly employed teacher at the academy

Fred enters the room, wearing a big backpack and carrying other bags.

Kathy : Can I help you?

Fred : Hi. I'm Fred, Fred Morgan.

Kathy : Ah, the new teacher, right? My boss just told me about you. I mean our boss. I'm Katherine, I'll be your supervisor here. Nice to meet you.

They shake hands.

Fred : Wow, your English is really good!

Kathy : Yeah…I'm from New York.

Fred : Oh, really? I thought…I mean…sorry, it's just that, you know, I figured that you were Korean.

Kathy : It's okay. Actually I was born here in Korea, in Gwangju, but I was adopted to the States when I was very young.

Fred : Oh, okay. I'm from New York, too, but my family doesn't live there anymore.

Kathy : Same here. Well, one of my sisters is still in New York, but the other one lives in Texas, and my parents moved to Florida after they retired.

Fred : Oh, wow, mine too! I mean, they did, but they passed away a few years back.

Kathy : Sorry to hear that. (beat) Hey, you look exhausted! Let me guess - you just got here, right?

Fred : Yeah, I left New York about two days ago, and I arrived in Incheon early this morning. So…I have been in Korea for a total of three hours!

Kathy : In that case, I guess you'd like to…freshen up a little? Let's go meet the boss, then I'll show you to your new apartment.

Fred : Sounds great. Let's go!

Translation

배경 : Super Duper 영어학원의 라운지

인물 : 영어학원 원어민 선생님들 중 책임자인 Katherine, 학원에 새로 온 사고뭉치 Fred

큰 배낭을 매고 다른 가방들을 들고 Fred가 방으로 들어온다.

Kathy: 도와드릴까요?

Fred : 안녕하세요. 저는 Fred, Fred Morgan입니다

Kathy: 아, 새로 오신 선생님, 맞죠? 원장선생님이 방금 당신에 관해 말씀했어요. 제 말은 우리들의 원장선생님이요. 나는 Katherine이예요. 나는 여기서 당신의 상관입니다. 만나서 반가워요.

그들은 악수를 한다.

Fred : 와, 당신의 영어는 매우 훌륭해요.

Kathy: 아... 난 뉴욕에서 왔어요.

Fred : 오, 정말요? 나는 단지... 내 말은... 미안해요. 당신이 알다시피 그냥 난 당신이 한국인이라고 생각했어요.

Kathy: 괜찮아요. 실제로 난 한국 광주에서 태어났어요. 하지만 내가 아주 어렸을 때 미국으로 입양되었어요.

Fred : 오, 그러셨구나. 나도 뉴욕에서 왔어요. 하지만 나의 가족들은 더 이상 그곳에서 살지 않아요.

Kathy: 저도 마찬가지예요. 나의 여동생 중 한 명은 아직 뉴욕에 있어요 하지만 다른 한 명은 텍사스에 살아요 그리고 나의 부모님들도 은퇴 후에 프로리다로 이사가셨어요.

Fred : 오, 와, 저도 그래요! 제 말은 제 부모님들도 그러셨어요. 그런데 몇 년 전에 돌아가셨지요.

Kathy: 유감이군요. 당신 몹시 지쳐 보여요. 맞춰볼까요? 당신 방금 여기 도착한 거 맞죠?

Fred : 네, 나는 이틀 전에 뉴욕 떠나서 인천에 오늘 아침 일찍 도착했어요. 그래서 한국에 온지 이제 세 시간되었죠.

Kathy: 그렇다면 좀 쉬는 게 좋지 않을까요? 원장선생님 만나러 가요 그리고 내가 당신의 새 아파트를 보여 드릴께요.

Fred : 네 좋아요. 갑시다!

Words & expressions

① I mean...	제 말은...
② it's just that...	그건 단지..
③ figure	판단하다
④ be adopted	입양되다
⑤ same here	저도 마찬가지입니다
⑥ retire	은퇴하다
⑦ pass away	돌아가시다
⑧ a few years back	몇 년 전에
⑨ exhausted	기진맥진한
⑩ let me guess...	제가 맞춰보죠
⑪ get (in the sense of 'arrive')	도착하다
⑫ in that case	그 경우엔
⑬ freshen up	몸단장을 하다

Comprehension questions

1. Where was Katherine born?
   a) Gwangju b) New York c) Texas d) Florida

2. Why is Fred surprised?
   a) Because he came too early.
   b) Because he hasn't been in Korea long.
   c) Because he didn't know Katherine was American.
   d) Because he didn't know Katherine was his supervisor.

3. When did Fred arrive in Korea?
   a) two days ago b) two hours ago
   c) three days ago d) three hours ago

WRITING PROCESS

How to format a paragraph

1. What is a paragraph?

A paragraph is a group of sentences about one topic. A topic is one, main idea.

Examples:
My Family
Friendship
My Pet
How to Play Soccer
Shopping for Clothes Online

1. 단락이란?

단락이란 한 주제에 관해서 쓴 문장들입니다. 주제는 하나의 중요한 아이디어입니다.

예시:
나의 가족
우정
나의 애완동물
축구하는 법
인터넷 옷 쇼핑

2. How do you format a paragraph?

There are some IMPORTANT rules to remember when writing a paragraph.

(1) Give your paragraph a TITLE.
(2) INDENT the first sentence of your paragraph about 1.25 cm in.
(3) BEGIN each sentence at the end of the sentence that comes before it. DON'T START each new sentence on a new line.
(4) WRITE the whole word on the next writing line if a word is too long to fit at the end of a line.

2. 단락 작성 법

한 단락을 쓸 때 몇 가지 중요한 규칙이 있습니다.

(1) 단락의 제목을 씁니다.
(2) 단락의 첫 문장은 1.25cm 들여 쓰기를 합니다.
(3) 하나의 문장이 끝나고 그 다음 문장을 이어서 씁니다. 새로운 문장을 새 줄에서 시작하면 안 됩니다.
(4) 한 단어가 그 줄에 다 들어가지 않으면, (단어를 끊어서 쓰지 말고) 그 단어 전체를 그 다음 줄에 씁니다.

3. Edited paragraph

My Classmate

My classmate's name is Miyoung Kim. She comes from Jeju, a small island south of the Korean peninsula. She moved to Seoul two years ago. She is single and lives with her younger sister. They grew up in the same city on Jeju, and they have been friends for fifteen years. This semester, Miyoung is studying English and Japanese. When she is not studying, she works in a bakery as a cashier. She likes her job, but sometimes the bakery is very busy and she gets tired. On weekends, she often goes bicycling along the Han River or hiking in the mountains around Seoul. She plans to become a tour guide. Miyoung has an exciting life, and she is looking forward to graduating from Cyber University.

나의 학급 친구

나의 학급 친구의 이름은 김미영입니다. 그녀는 제주도에서 왔습니다. 그곳은 한국의 남쪽에 위치한 작은 섬입니다. 그녀는 2년 전에 서울로 이사 왔습니다. 그녀는 미혼이고, 그녀의 여동생과 함께 삽니다. 그들은 제주도에서 함께 성장하였습니다 그리고 그들은 15년 동안 친구로 지냈습니다. 이번 학기에, 미영이는 영어와 일본어를 공부합니다. 그녀가 공부하지 않을 때에는, 그녀는 제과점에서 출납원으로 일을 합니다. 그녀는 그녀의 일을 좋아합니다. 하지만 때때로 제과점이 너무 바빠서 피곤해지기도 합니다. 주말에 그녀는 자주 한강 근처에서 자전거를 타거나 서울 근처의 산을 오르기도 합니다. 그녀는 나중에 관광 가이드가 되려고 합니다. 미영이는 즐겁게 지내고 있고, 사이버대학교 졸업을 고대하고 있습니다.

4. What does the writing process look like?

Good writing involves THINKING, PLANNING, CHECKING, and REVISING.

Good writers follow these 4 steps:

(1) Prewriting- Brainstorming and outlining
(2) Writing the first draft
(3) Editing the first draft
(4) Writing the final draft to hand in to the teacher.

In the next tasks, you will follow Eunha Jang as she goes through the first step toward writing a paragraph about her mother.

4. 작문과정은 어떠한가?

좋은 글쓰기는 생각, 계획, 검토 그리고 수정을 거치게 됩니다.

좋은 작가는 4가지 과정을 따릅니다:

(1) Pre-writing - 본격적인 글쓰기 전에 브레인 스토밍과 개요 작성하기
(2) 초안 쓰기
(3) 초안 편집하기
(4) 최종 원고 쓰기

다음 tasks에서 당신은 장은하가 그녀의 엄마에 대해 쓰기 위해서 첫 단계 작성을 어떻게 하는 지 보게 될 것입니다.

Task 1 Pre-writing

은하는 그녀의 어머니에 관해서 브레인 스토밍을 하였습니다. 주제와 직접적인 관련성이 없어서 지워야 하는 문장이나 구에 체크 표시 하시오. (주의: 주제는 그녀의 '어머니' 입니다. 그녀의 어머니와 관련되지 않은 것은 없애야 합니다.)

- Kind, average-height, was a stay-at-home mom. (   )
- Now she works at a clothing store (   )
- 50 years old, born on July 1, 1961 (   )
- Lives in Busan with my father, born in Changwon Province (   )
- Grew up in the countryside, grew up poor (   )
- Helped on the family farm. Picked crops with her brother (   )
- Her grandmother passed away when she was in high school. She was kind. (   )
- Her brother became a businessman. He works for Samsung. (   )
- He has two children (   )
- I want my mother and father to move to Seoul. (   )
- Patient. Never scolded me when I did poorly at school (   )
- My father was very strict. (   )
- Liked to play the piano. Taught me when I was little (   )
- On the weekends, she hikes, shops, and spends time with friends. (   )
- Sometimes, she visits me and my brother. (   )
- She takes care of my father. (   )
- Soon he will retire. He wants to travel one day. (   )

Task 2 Outlining activity

다음으로, 은하는 개요를 작성하고자 합니다. 이 작업을 통해서 그녀는 어머니에 대해 쓴 문장들을 정리하게 됩니다. 각 박스에 올바른 문장들을 넣으시오. 박스 1은 이미 완성되어 있습니다.

Kind, average-height, was a stay-at-home mom
Now she works at a clothing store
50 years old, born on July 1, 1961
Lives in Busan with my father
Born in Changwon City
Grew up in the countryside, grew up poor
Helped on the family farm.
Picked crops with her brother
Patient. Never scolded me when I did poorly at school.
Lliked to play the piano. Taught me when I was little.
On the weekends, she hikes, shops, and spends time with friends.
Sometimes, she visits me and my brother.
She takes care of my father

1. She'd like to first introduce her mother.

50 years old, born on July 1, 1961
Lives in Pusan with my father
Born in Changwon City

2. Next, she'd like to describe her mother's childhood.

3. Then, she'd like to describe her own childhood memories of her mother.

4. Lastly, she'd like to describe her mother now.

GRAMMAR

Sentences and fragments

What is a sentence?

A sentence is a group of words that includes a subject and a verb and expresses a complete thought.

These are sentences:

1. He is an engineer.
2. It's pretty hot today.

3. She looks happy.
4. Are you hungry?
5. The man bought a new bicycle.
6. Where did you meet her?

These are not sentences:

1. Is an engineer.
2. Hot weather.
3. The man bought.
4. Because it snowed.

문장이란?

문장은 주어와 동사를 포함한 단어로 이루어져 있고, 완성된 생각을 표현합니다.

문장들:

1. 그는 엔지니어입니다.
2. 오늘은 매우 덥습니다.
3. 그녀는 행복해 보입니다.
4. 당신은 배가 고픕니까?
5. 남자는 새 자전거를 샀습니다.
6. 당신은 그녀를 어디서 만났습니까?

문장이 아닌 것들:

1. 엔지니어입니다
2. 더운 날씨
3. 남자는 샀습니다.
4. 눈이 오기 때문에

Task 3 Sentence or fragment?

다음을 읽고 완성된 문장이면 "S"에 문장의 일부이면 "F"에 표시하시오.

	S	F
1. Our new teacher from Long Island.	_____	_____
2. He just arrived in Korea.	_____	_____
3. Is very tall.	_____	_____
4. Katherine and three sisters.	_____	_____
5. She likes.	_____	_____
6. Hurry!	_____	_____

Task 4 Introducing yourself

먼저, 아래 질문 각각에 대한 간단한 대답을 적은 후, 그 대답을 이용해서 짧은 단락을 쓰시오.

1) What is your name?

____

2) When and where were you born?

____

3) How many people are there in your family?

____

4) What kind of personality do you have?

____

5) What do you do like to do in your free time?

____

6) Why are you studying at CUFS?

____

7) What do you want to do in the future?

____

Paragraph

WRAP-UP

1. Introducing ourselves and others
2. What is a paragraph?
3. How do you format a paragraph?
4. What does the writing process look like?
   1) Prewriting: Brainstorming and outlining
   2) Writing the first draft
   3) Editing the first draft
   4) Writing the final draft
5. Sentences and fragments

1. 자신과 다른 사람들을 소개하기
2. 단락은 무엇인가?
3. 단락은 어떻게 작성하는가?
4. 쓰기 과정은 어떠한가?
   1) 쓰기 전 과정: 브레인스토밍과 개요
   2) 초안 쓰기
   3) 초안 수정하기
   4) 최종 원고 쓰기
5. 문장과 문장의 일부

Unit 2

Introducing Ourselves and Others II

INTRODUCTION

Topic: Introducing ourselves and others
Writing Process: Editing a paragraph
Sentence Structure: Simple sentences, connecting words
Grammar: Punctuation, capitalization

주제: 우리자신과 다른 사람들 소개하기
글쓰기: 단락 수정
문장구조: 단문, 연결어
문법: 구두점, 대문자

WRITING PROCESS

1. Unedited paragraph

My New Teacher

My teacher's name is Fred Morgan.
My old teacher went back to England last week.
Fred is American, and he grew up in a small town outside New York City.

He has big voice.
He wants to learn how to speak Korean, but right now he only knows a few words, and his pronunciation is funny.
Before he came to Korea, Fred was a high school teacher in America.
He enjoys eating at Korean restaurants because he loves to eat spicy food.
I am hungry. I want to eat some rice right now!
In his free time, Fred likes to ride his bicycle along the Han River and go to baseball games.
I prefer soccer to baseball.
His favorite team is the Doosan Bears.
I like my new teacher. Because he is the teacher like a friend.
I hope he stays in Korea forever!

2. Edited paragraph

My New Teacher → **Center the title.**

Indent the first sentence.

My teacher's name is Fred Morgan. ~~My old teacher went back to England last week~~. Fred is American, and he grew up in a small town outside New York City. ~~He has big voice~~ **His voice is very deep.** He wants to learn how to speak Korean, but right now he only knows a few words, and his pronunciation is funny. Before he came to Korea, Fred was a high school teacher in America. He enjoys eating at Korean restaurants because he loves to eat spicy food. ~~I am hungry. I want to eat some rice right now!~~ In his free time, Fred likes to ride his bicycle along the Han River and go to baseball games. ~~I prefer soccer to baseball.~~

b

His favorite team is the Doosan Bears. I like my new teacher~~.~~ ~~B~~ecause

more like a friend than a teacher

he is ~~the teacher like a friend~~. I hope he stays in Korea forever!

3. Final paragraph

My New Teacher

My teacher's name is Fred Morgan. Fred is American, and he grew up in a small town outside New York City. His voice is very deep. He wants to learn how to speak Korean, but right now he only knows a few words, and his pronunciation is funny. Before he came to Korea, Fred was a high school teacher in America. He enjoys eating at Korean restaurants because he loves to eat spicy food. In his free time, Fred likes to ride his bicycle along the Han River and go to baseball games. His favorite team is the Doosan Bears. I like my new teacher because he is more like a friend than a teacher. I hope he stays in Korea forever!

나의 새로운 선생님

나의 새로운 선생님의 이름은 Fred Morgan입니다. Fred는 미국인이고, 그는 뉴욕시 외곽의 작은 마을에서 성장했습니다. 그의 목소리는 힘이 있습니다. 그는 한국어로 말하는 것을 배우고 싶어하지만 현재 그는 몇 마디만 압니다. 그리고 그의 발음은 웃깁니다. 한국에 오기 전에 Fred는 미국에서 고등학교 교사였습니다. 그는 매운 음식을 아주 좋아하기 때문에 한국식당에서 음식을 먹는 것을 즐깁니다. 시간이 있을 때, Fred는 한강을 따라 자전거를 타고 야구경기를 보러 가는 것을 좋아합니다. 저는 야구보다 축구를 더 좋아합니다. 그가 가장 좋아하는 팀은 두산 베어스입니다. 그는 친구처럼 느껴지기 때문에 나는 새로운 선생님을 좋아합니다. 저는 그가 한국에 영원히 머무르길 희망합니다.

Task 1 Editing awkward expressions

다음 단락을 읽고 밑줄 친 부분을 적절한 표현으로 바꾸시오.

Oh, (1) I am so poor! When I (2) go school every day, I always have a few pimples on my face. This is important because everybody (3) has a complex towards their own face. When I lose confidence in (4) oneself, I feel terrible at school. Then, after I (5) go to home I go to my room and cry for a long time. This is not the only thing that I am worried about, but it is the biggest.

(1) I am so poor! → ______________________!

(2) go school → ______________________

(3) has a complex towards their → ______________________

(4) oneself → ______________________

(5) go to home → ______________________

SENTENCE STRUCTURE

Simple sentences and connecting words

A sentence is a group of words that expresses a complete thought. There are many types of sentences (e.g., simple, compound, complex sentences, etc). We will study simple sentences and connecting words today.

1. Simple sentences

A simple sentence has one subject-verb combination.

The subject or the verb in a simple sentence may be compound. Compound means that there are two or more subjects or verbs in the sentence.

SS+V or S+VV

(1) S+V

*My older **brother** speaks English well.* (S= brother; V=speaks)

*In the mornings, the **traffic** is bad.* (S= traffic; V=is)

(2) SS+V

*My **mother** and **father** live in Busan.* (S1= mother; S2=father; V=live)

***Jack** and **Haemin** are usually happy children.* (S1=Jack; S2=Haemin; V=are)

(3) S+VV

*My **friend** <u>is working</u> and <u>going</u> to school at the same time.* (S= friend; V1=is working; V2=(is) going)
*The **president** of Korea <u>traveled</u> to Canada and <u>visited</u> with the Canadian Prime Minister last month.* (S= president; V1=traveled; V2=visited)

(4) SS+VV

*My **classmate** and **I** <u>worked</u> on homework and <u>went</u> for drinks after.* (S1= classmate; S2=I; V1=worke; V2=went)
*Next semester, **CUFS** and **HUFS** <u>will have</u> a festival and <u>hold</u> a friendly soccer tournament.* (S1=CUFS; S2=HUFS; V1=will have; V2= (will) hold)

하나의 문장은 완성된 생각을 표현하는 단어들의 그룹입니다. 여러 종류의 문장이 있습니다 (즉, 단문, 중문, 복문 등). 오늘은 단문과 연결어를 공부해 보도록 합니다.

1. 단문

단문은 하나의 주어와 동사로 구성되어 있습니다.
단문 중에는 주어나 동사가 복합적인 형태를 갖는 것도 있습니다. 복합적인 형태란 두 개나 그 이상의 주어나 동사가 있다는 것을 의미합니다. SS+V 또는 S+VV

(1) S+V

나의 형은 영어를 잘합니다.
오전에는 교통상황이 좋지 않습니다.

(2) SS+V

나의 어머니와 아버지는 부산에 사십니다.
Jack과 혜민은 대개 행복한 어린이들입니다.

(3) S+VV

나의 친구는 일하면서 동시에 학교에서 공부하고 있습니다.
지난 달 한국 대통령은 캐나다로 가서 캐나다 총리를 만났습니다.

(4) SS+VV

저의 학급친구와 저는 숙제를 한 후 술을 마시러 나갔습니다.
다음 학기에 CUFS와 HUFS는 축제를 함께 열고 친선 축구경기를 가질 예정입니다.

2. Connecting words: and, but, or

Connecting words are conjunctions.
The most common connecting words are *and, but,* and *or*.

And
Shopping and hiking are my favorite weekend activities.
He has class on Mondays, Wednesdays, and Fridays.

But
They tried hard but failed to win.
My parents are very old but still energetic.

Or (connects two or more similar things in negative sentences)
They don't like beef or chicken.

She can't play piano, cook, or sew very well.

Or (connects two or more choices or alternatives)
We would like to go to Jeju-Do, Boracay, or Tokyo during our next summer vacation.
(We cannot go to all three places. We will choose one.)

2. 연결어: and, but, or

연결어는 일종의 접속사입니다.
가장 흔한 연결어는 and와 or 입니다.

그리고
쇼핑과 하이킹은 내가 가장 좋아하는 주말 활동입니다.
그는 월요일, 수요일 그리고 금요일에 수업이 있습니다.

그러나
그들은 열심히 노력했으나 이기지 못했습니다.
나의 부모님은 많이 연로하시지만 여전히 활동적이십니다.

또는 (부정문에서 두 개 이상의 비슷한 것을 연결할 때)
그들은 소고기나 닭고기를 좋아하지 않습니다.
그녀는 피아노 연주, 요리, 또는 바느질을 잘 하지 못합니다.

또는 (두 개 이상의 선택이나 대체물을 연결할 때)
우리는 다음 여름방학기간 동안 제주도, Boracay 또는 Tokyo에 가고 싶습니다.
(우리는 모든 장소를 갈 수 없습니다. 우리는 한 개만 선택할 수 있습니다.)

Task 2

다음 단락을 이루는 각 단문의 패턴을 파악하고 아래 보기 중에서 그 패턴을 고르시오.

Example:

My grandmother loves to play chess and lets me play with her.

(1) SV (2) SVV (3) SSV (4) SSVV

Answer: (2)

*My **grandmother** loves to play chess and lets me play with her.*

SVV (S= grandmother; V1=loves; V2=lets)

My Grandmother

My grandmother is over 80 years old but is very active for her age. She and my grandfather have known each other for over 70 years and have been married for 60 years. They have three children, five grandchildren, and 4 great-grandchildren. My grandmother loves parties and invites the entire family over for dinner once a month. At these family gatherings, she cooks for us and even bakes us a cake and cookies. She is never too tired to stay up and tell us stories half the night.

1. *My grandmother is over 80 years old but is very active for her age.*

(1) SV (2) SSV (3) SVV (4) SSVV

2. *She and my grandfather have known each other for over 70 years and have been married for 60 years.*
(1) SV (2) SSV (3) SVV (4) SSVV

3. *They have three children, five grandchildren, and 4 great-grandchildren.*
(1) SV (2) SSV (3) SVV (4) SSVV

4. *My grandmother loves parties and invites the entire family over for dinner once a month.*
(1) SV (2) SSV (3) SVV (4) SSVV

5. *At these family gatherings, she cooks for us and even bakes us a cake and cookies.*
(1) SV (2) SSV (3) SVV (4) SSVV

6. *She is never too tired to stay up and tell us stories half the night.*
(1) SV (2) SSV (3) SVV (4) SSVV

Task 3

다음 단어들을 순서에 맞게 배열하여 단문을 만드시오.

Example:

SVV: works part-time My older brother goes college to and
→ My older brother goes to college and works part-time./
My older brother works part-time and goes to college.

1. SV: My sleeps next to my bed on the floor dog

____

2. SVV: don't have school on Mondays We or Taekwondo lessons take

____

3. SSVV: fly to Hawaii would like to My sister walk on the beaches and I and

____

Task 4

다음 짝지은 두 문장을 and 혹은 or를 써서 연결하시오. 같은 단어를 반복하여 쓰지 않도록 주의하시오.

Example:

I like soup. I like salad.
I like soup and salad. O
I like soup and like salad. X (☹ *very repetitive*)

1. Bora can speak Japanese. She can understand Japanese.

____

2. Jimin can't speak Chinese. She can't speak Thai.

____

3. Green is my favorite color. White is my favorite color. (Remember: color → colors)

____

4. Her English is strongly accented. Her English is intelligible.

____

5. I might have beer. I might have wine. I might have juice. (I will have only one of these drinks.)

____

GRAMMAR

Punctuation & capitalization

1. Punctuation

A sentence ends with a period(.), a question mark(?), or an exclamation point(!)

I have lived in a big city since I was born.
Are you married or single?
What a big boy you've become!

1. 구두점

문장 끝에는 마침표(.), 물음표(?), 또는 느낌표(!)가 옵니다.

나는 태어나서부터 줄곧 대도시에 살고 있습니다.
결혼하셨습니까? 아니면 미혼이신가요?
아이구 너 다 컸구나!

2. Capitalization

(1) The first word in a sentence

You look unhappy.
What's the matter?

(2) The pronoun

Hello. Could I speak to Michelle?
When I watch movies, I eat popcorn.

(3) Names of people and their titles, and places

Katherine
Professor Indiana Jones
Mr. and Mrs. Smith
North Africa
the Hilton Hotel

(4) Nationalities, religions, languages, and ethnic groups

He's Russian.
They are studying Chinese history
She's Christian.

I speak French.

He's Native American.

(5) Names of days, months, and public holidays (but not seasons of the year!)

Saturday

February

Easter

Thanksgiving

(X) Summer

(6) Acronyms

FBI

NBA

UNESCO

DPRK

(7) Titles (except for prepositions, conjunctions, articles, etc. that don't come first)

Gone with the Wind

War and Peace

The Good, the Bad, and the Weird

Journey to the West

2. 대문자 사용

(1) 문장에서 첫 번째 단어

당신 기분이 안 좋아 보입니다.

무슨 일 있습니까?

(2) 대명사

안녕하세요. Michelle과 통화할 수 있을까요?
저는 영화를 볼 때 팝콘을 먹습니다.

(3) 사람의 이름과 그들의 직함, 장소

Katherine
Indiana Jones교수
Smith 씨와 Smith 부인
북아프리카
Hilton 호텔

(4) 국적, 종교, 언어, 그리고 민족

그는 러시아인입니다.
그들은 중국 역사를 공부하고 있습니다.
그녀는 기독교인입니다.
저는 프랑스어로 말합니다.
그는 미국 원주민입니다.

(5) 일, 월, 공휴일의 이름 (그러나 계절은 아님!)

토요일
2월
부활절
추수감사절
(X) 여름

(6) 머리글자로 만든 말

FBI (Federal Bureau of Investigation: 미국 연방 수사국)
NBA (National Basketball Association: 미국 프로 농구 협회)
UNESCO (United Nations Educational, Scientific and Cultural Organization: 국제연합 교육과학문화기구, 유네스코)

DPRK (the Democratic People's Republic of Korea: 조선민주주의 인민 공화국, 북한)

(7) 영화, 책 등의 제목
(처음에 나오지는 않는 전치사, 접속사, 관사 등은 제외)

Gone with the Wind (바람과 함께 사라지다)
War and Peace (전쟁과 평화)
The Good, the Bad, and the Weird (놈놈놈)
Journey to the West (서유기)

Task 5 Punctuation

각 문장을 읽고, 적절한 구두점을 마지막에 쓰시오. – 마침표(.), 물음표(?), 또는 느낌표(!)

1. How long have you been in Korea ______
2. Help, I am being robbed ______
3. Korea has four seasons ______
4. You've been to New York before, haven't you ______
5. Call an ambulance ______
6. She asked me where to go ______
7. Oh no, he's got a gun ______

Task 6 Capitalization

다음 단락을 읽고 대문자로 써야 하는 단어를 찾아서 대문자로 고쳐 쓰시오.

my name is Cha, Du-ri, and i have had an exciting life. I am a professional footballer player for the scottish Premier League club celtic. My father, Cha, bum-kun, played in the 1986 World Cup, and I played in 2010. that means I am the first Korean and the only asian player to have played in a fifa World Cup as a second generation player. I was proud to represent my country on the world stage.

1. ____________________
2. ____________________
3. ____________________
4. ____________________
5. ____________________
6. ____________________
7. ____________________

WRAP-UP

1. Editing a paragraph
2. Simple sentences: S+V, SS+V, S+VV, SS+VV
3. Connecting words: and, but, or
4. Punctuation: a period, a question mark, an exclamation point
5. Capitalization

1. 단락 수정하기
2. 단문: S+V, SS+V, S+VV, SS+VV
3. 연결어: and, but, or
4. 구두점: 마침표, 물음표, 느낌표
5. 대문자 사용

Unit 3

Living from Day to Day I

INTRODUCTION

Topic: Living from day to day
Writing Process: Time-order paragraphs
Grammar: Comma rules I

주제: 하루하루 살아가기
글쓰기: 시간순서에 따른 단락
문법과 구두점: 콤마 규칙 I

OUR LIFE

Setting: a café nearby Super Duper English Academy
Characters: Katherine, Fred

Kathy : So, you've been in Korea for nearly two weeks already. How is everything going?
Fred : Wow, has it only been two weeks? It feels like forever!
Kathy : Yeah, I know what you mean. What have you been up to so far?

Fred : Well, besides teaching I've been exploring Seoul, trying new foods, meeting new people, visiting palaces···you know, stuff like that. Why, what do you usually do?

Kathy : I've pretty much settled into a standard daily routine. I wake up every morning at 6:00 sharp and go for a jog down by the river. After that I teach from 8-12, then grab some lunch and head to class.

Fred : Class? What are you studying?

Kathy : I'm taking a Korean class over at HUFS. It's really great - you should give it a try!

Fred : Yeah, you're right. The other day I was in kind of a sticky situation and I couldn't understand what anybody was saying to me.

Kathy : Oh no, what happened?

Fred : Well, after a long bike ride I decided to try the bath house near my apartment, but when I got into the tub, these guys got angry and starting yelling at me. I had no idea what they were talking about, so I just jumped out and went home.

Kathy : Hmm···did you remember to wash yourself off before getting into the bath?

Fred : Wash myself before getting into the bath? What do you mean?

Kathy : Well, Koreans bathe differently from Americans. You have to take a shower before you get into the bath, so the bath water stays clean for everyone else.

Fred : Ah···.actually yeah, that makes sense! Oh man, I really need to sign up for that Korean class!

Translation

배경 : Super Duper 영어학원 근처의 까페

인물 : Katherine, Fred

Kathy: 그럼 벌써 한국에서 지낸 지가 거의 2주정도 지냈네요. 어때요?

Fred : 와! 겨우 2주였나요? 아주 오랜 시간인 것 같은 느낌이네요!

Kathy: 그래요, 무슨 뜻인지 알아요. 지금까지 어떻게 지냈어요?

Fred : 물론, 가르치는 것 외에 서울을 답사하고, 새로운 음식을 시도하고, 새로운 사람을 만나고, 명소들을 방문하고......당신이 아는 그런 것들이요. 왜요, 당신은 주로 무엇을 하나요?

Kathy: 저는 거의 틀에 박힌 생활을 하고 있어요. 매일 아침 6시 정각에 일어나서 저 아래 강을 따라 조깅을 하죠. 그 후에 8시에서 12시까지 가르치고 그 후, 점심을 간단히 먹고 수업을 받으러 가요.

Fred : 수업이요? 무슨 공부를 하고 계시죠?

Kathy: 저는 HUFS에서 한국어 수업을 듣습니다. 정말 좋아요– 당신도 한번 들어보세요!

Fred : 네, 그래요. 지난번 저는 힘든 일을 겪었고 누군가 나에게 한 말을 이해할 수 없었죠.

Kathy: 아, 무슨 일이었죠?

Fred : 음, 긴 시간 자전거를 탄 후 저는 저의 아파트 근처 목욕탕에서 목욕하기로 했어요. 하지만 제가 탕에 들어갔을 때, 그들은 화를 냈고, 내게 소리를 질렀어요. 저는 그들이 무슨 말을 하는 지 전혀 알 수 없었어요. 그래서 저는 그냥 뛰쳐나와 집으로 갔습니다.

Kathy: 음...... 당신은 탕에 들어가기 전에 샤워를 해야 하는 걸 알고 있나요?

Fred : 탕에 들어가기 전에 샤워를 한다? 그게 무슨 말이죠?

Kathy: 그러니까, 한국인들은 미국인들과는 다르게 목욕합니다. 탕에 들어가기 전에 샤워를 해야 합니다. 그래야 다른 사람들 모두 깨끗한 목욕물에 들어갈 수가 있죠.

Fred : 아 정말 그렇네요, 그거 말 되네요! 이런, 나야말로 정말 한국어 수업을 꼭 들어야겠네요!

Words & expressions

① feels like forever	아주 오래된 것처럼 느껴지다
② What have you been up to?	어떻게 지내셨습니까?
③ you know	당신도 알다시피
④ stuff (in reference to activities)	~것들(활동에 대한 언급)
⑤ pretty much	거의
⑥ settle into a routine	틀에 박힌 생활에 적응하다
⑦ 6:00 sharp	6시 정각
⑧ grab some (breakfast/lunch/ dinner/a snack/a drink)	아침/점심/저녁/간식/음료를 급히 먹다/마시다
⑨ head (= go)	가다
⑩ over at...	(저쪽) ~에서
⑪ give it a try	한 번 시도해 보다
⑫ kind of	일종의
⑬ a sticky situation	힘든, 어려운 상황
⑭ Oh man!	이런!

Comprehension questions

1. What is the order of Katherine's daily routine?
   a) jog → teach → lunch → Korean class
   b) teach → Korean class → lunch → jog
   c) lunch → teach → jog → Korean class
   d) Korean class → lunch → jog → teach

2. Which of the following is NOT one of Fred's normal activities?
   a) dining
   b) socializing
   c) sightseeing
   d) volunteering

3. Katherine and Fred's words imply that __________.
   a) Americans don't take baths
   b) Americans don't clean themselves before they take a bath
   c) Americans shower in the morning, not in the evening
   d) Americans are dirtier than Koreans

WRITING PROCESS

Time-order paragraphs

In this unit, you will learn how to give instructions. You will explain how to do something—how to plan a party, how to get to your house, how to change a tire—and how to make something—how to make kimchi, cookies, traditional Korean fans, rice cake and so on. To do this, you will explain each step of your instructions in order by time. At the end, you will write a time-order paragraph.

시간순서에 따른 단락

이 단원에서는, 지침을 제공하는 방법을 배우게 됩니다. 당신은 무언가를 하는 방법에 대해 설명할 것입니다. – 파티를 계획하는 법, 당신의 집까지 가는 법, 타이어를 교환하는 법 등. 그리고 무언가를 만드는 법에 대해 설명할 것입니다. – 김치, 쿠키, 한국의 전통부채, 떡 등을 만드는 법. 이렇게 하려면, 당신은 시간순서에 따라 각 단계에 대해서 설명해야 합니다. 마지막으로 당신은 시간순서에 따른 하나의 단락을 쓰게 됩니다.

1. Time-order paragraphs

In time-order paragraphs, ideas are put in order by time. For example, when you write about your evening activities, you use time order to tell about it. You write *first...next...and then....last....*

When you write instructions, you divide them up into a series of steps in order by time. For example, when you teach someone to make ramen, you explain how to boil the water before you tell them when to add the ingredients.

Below is a paragraph written by Dori Lee. She is a first-year student at CUFS.

1. 시간순서에 따른 단락

시간순서 단락에서, 아이디어는 시간에 순서에 따라서 나열될 것입니다. 예를 들어, 당신이 저녁 활동에 대하여 쓸 때, 시간 순서대로 쓰면 됩니다. 당신은 먼저..... 다음에...... 그리고 나서...... 마지막으로...... 라고 씁니다.

당신이 지침을 쓸 때, 당신은 시간에 따라 순서대로, 몇 개의 단계로 나눕니다. 예를 들어, 어떤 사람에게 라면을 끓이는 법을 가르칠 때, 재료를 언제 넣는가를 말하기 전에 물을 끓이는 방법에 대해 설명합니다.

아래는 이 도리 학생이 쓴 단락입니다. 그녀는 CUFS 1학년 학생입니다.

2. Model paragraph

Dori Lee

How to Choose Classes

Choosing the right classes each semester can be stressful, but you can reduce your stress by following these steps. The first step is to become familiar with the graduation requirements of your major. A good idea is to go to your department's page that deals with your major and memorize the requirements. Second, plan, plan, plan. Write out a program to make sure you have all the courses you need for graduation including prerequisites—classes you must pass before you can register for them. The third step is to talk with as many older students as you can for advice on which courses to take. Try to avoid wasting time and money. Fourth, register for each class as soon as you can. Waiting even an hour may mean that the classes you want or need are filled. To sum up, plan ahead to avoid missing any required classes, to avoid bad classes, and to graduate on time.

이 도리

수업을 선택하는 방법

매 학기 적절한 수업을 선택하는 것은 스트레스를 받을 수 있는 일이지만, 다음 단계를 따라서 하면 스트레스를 줄일 수 있습니다. 첫 번째 단계는 전공과 관련된 졸업 요건에 익숙해지는 것입니다. 이것을 위해 좋은 방법은 전공 학과 페이지로 가서 필요한 요건을 기억해 두는 것입니다. 둘째, 계획하고, 계획하고, 또 계획해야 합니다. 졸업에 필요한 모든 과정을 이수할 수 있도록 매 학기 프로그램을 작성하십시오. 일부 수업은 당신이 등록하기 전에 들어야 하는 선수과목이 필요할 수도 있습니다. 세 번째 단계는 어떤 수업을 들어야 하는지 되도록 많은 선배들과 이야기하는 것입니다. 시간과 돈을 낭비하지 않도록 노력하십시오. 넷째, 가능한 빨리 각 수업을 수강신청 하십시오. 심지어 한 시간을 기다리면 당신이 원하거나 필요로 하는 수업이 다 찰 수도 있습니다. 요약하면, 필수 과목을 놓치지 않고, 좋지 않은 수업은 피하고, 제 기간에 졸업하도록 미리 계획을 세우십시오.

3. Planning a paragraph: outlining

Before you write a paragraph, you should plan what you are going to write. A plan for a writing assignment is called an outline. An outline helps you organize your ideas and put them in logical order. You will now learn how to make an outline. The first step is to get ideas by prewriting.

당신이 단락을 작성하기 전에, 당신이 무엇을 쓸 것인지 계획해야 합니다. 작문 과제에 대한 계획을 개요라고 합니다. 개요는 당신이 아이디어를 정리하고 논리적인 순서에 맞게 배열하도록 하는데 도움을 줍니다. 이제 개요를 작성하는 방법을 배우게 됩니다. 첫 번째 단계는 prewriting을 통해 아이디어를 얻는 것입니다.

Step 1: Brainstorm to get ideas

Dori's first step in writing her paragraph was to get ideas by prewriting. She brainstormed what to do when choosing classes before the start of the semester.

How to Choose Classes

Find out which classes you need to graduate.
Make a list of classes to take each semester.
Read your department's course listings and requirements for your major.
Register for your classes early.
Work a part-time job.
Find out about prerequisite classes.

Talk to older students for advice on classes.
Talk to as many older students as you can.
Which classes are good?
Which classes are bad?
Plan a lot.

도리의 첫 번째 단계는 prewriting으로 아이디어를 얻는 것입니다. 그녀는 학기 시작 전에 수업을 선택할 때 어떻게 해야 할지 브레인스토밍 했습니다.

수업선택을 하는 방법

졸업에 필요한 수업을 알아보십시오.
매 학기 들어야 할 수업의 목록을 만드십시오.
학과 코스 목록과 전공 필수조건을 읽으십시오.
일찍 수강신청을 하십시오.
아르바이트를 하십시오.
선수 과목에 대해 알아보십시오
수업에 대한 조언을 얻기 위해 선배들과 얘기를 나누십시오.
가능한 많은 선배들과 이야기하십시오.
어떤 수업이 괜찮나요?
어떤 수업이 나쁜가요?
많은 계획을 세우십시오.

Step 2: Edit the brainstorming list

After brainstorming your list, the next step is to edit it. Decide what you want to include in your final paragraph and what you want to omit. In addition to this, you want to do the following:

- Combine ideas that belong together.
- Cross out repeated ideas.
- Cross out ideas not directly related to the main idea. The main idea here is *how to choose your classes*.

Now, take a look at how Dori edited her brainstorming list.

How to Choose Classes

- Find out which classes you need to graduate.
- Make a list of classes to take each semester.
- Read your department's course listings and requirements for your major.
- Register for your classes early.
- ~~Work a part-time job.~~
- Find out about prerequisite classes.
- Talk to older students for advice on classes.
- ~~Talk to as many older students as you can.~~
- Which classes are good?
- Which classes are bad?
- Plan a lot.

목록을 브레인스토밍한 후, 다음 단계는 그것을 수정하는 것입니다. 마지막에 단락에 포함시킬 것과 단락에서 뺄 것을 결정해야 합니다. 그리고 또한 다음과 같은 것을 해야 합니다:

- 연관된 아이디어를 합친다.
- 반복되는 아이디어를 선을 그어서 지운다.
- 주요 아이디어와 관련이 없는 아이디어를 선을 그어서 지운다. 여기에서 주요 아이디어는 수업을 선택하는 방법이다.

이제 Dori가 브레인스토밍한 목록을 어떻게 수정했는지 봅시다.

- 졸업에 필요한 수업을 알아보십시오.
- 매 학기 들어야 할 수업의 목록을 만드십시오.
- 학과 코스 목록과 전공 필수조건을 읽으십시오.
- 일찍 수강신청을 하십시오.
- ~~아르바이트를 하십시오.~~
- 선수 과목에 대해서 알아보십시오.
- 수업에 대한 조언을 얻기 위해 선배들과 얘기를 나누십시오.
- ~~가능한 많은 선배들과 이야기하십시오.~~
- 어떤 수업이 괜찮나요?
- 어떤 수업이 나쁜가요?
- 많은 계획을 세우십시오.

Step 3: Organize the list

The third step is to put each step in your list in order. In Dori's list, each step is given a capital letter (A, B, C, etc.). She also includes a title and a topic sentence.

(Title) How to Choose Classes

(Topic sentence) Choosing the right classes each semester can be stressful, but you can reduce your stress by following these steps.

A. Become familiar with the graduation requirements of your major.
B. Plan a lot.
C. Talk with as many older students as you can.
D. Register for each class as soon as you can.

세 번째 단계는 목록의 각 단계를 순서대로 배열하는 것입니다. 도리의 목록에서, 각 단계에는 대문자(A, B, C, 등)가 제공됩니다. 또한 제목과 주제 문장을 포함하고 있습니다.

(제목) 수업을 선택하는 방법

(주제 문장) 매 학기 올바른 수업을 선택해야 하는 것 때문에 때로 스트레스를 받기도 하지만, 다음 단계를 따라감으로써 여러분은 스트레스를 줄일 수 있습니다.

A. 전공의 졸업 요건에 익숙해지십시오.
B. 많은 계획을 세우십시오.
C. 가능한 많은 선배들과 이야기를 나누십시오
D. 가능한 한 빨리 각 과목의 수강신청을 하십시오.

Task 1 Multiple choices

각 문제를 읽고 올바른 답을 고르시오.

1. Which of the following is an idea that should be included in Dori's paragraph on "How to Choose Classes"?
   a) Have fun while going to college.
   b) Read your department's course listings and requirements for your major.
   c) Read as many books as possible.
   d) Take time to choose the right person.

2. Choose two of the following that mean the same thing.
   a) prerequisite classes
   b) homework
   c) classes you should have taken.
   d) plan a lot

3. What can students learn by asking older peers about classes?
   a) Whether the classes are good.
   b) Whether the classes are bad.
   c) Whether they should graduate.
   d) both a & b

Task 2 Revising your list

아래에서 "수업을 선택하는 방법"에 대해서 도리가 쓴 단락에 포함될 필요가 없는 세 개의 아이디어를 고르시오.

a. Find out the classes you need to graduate.
b. Make a list of classes to take each semester.
c. Read your department's course listings and requirements for your major.
d. Register for your classes early.
e. Work a part-time job.
f. Find out about used bookstores.
g. Find out about prerequisite classes.
h. Talk to older students for advice on classes.
i. Which classes are good?
j. Which classes are bad?
k. Play a lot.

____________ ____________ ____________

Task 3 Organizing the list

"수업을 선택하는 방법"에 대한 글을 쓸 때, 다음 아이디어를 올바른 순서대로 나열한 것을 고르시오.

A. Plan a lot
B. Talk with as many older students as you can.
C. Become familiar with the graduation requirements of your major.
D. Register for each class as soon as you can.

a. (A, B, C, D)
b. (B, A, C, D)
c. (D, C, A, B)
d. (C, A, B, D)

GRAMMAR

Comma rules I

Commas: three rules

1. Put a comma after time-order expressions such as *First, Next, After that, Before going to Grandma's house*, etc..

Examples:

- First, pour the rice in a bowl.
- After that, turn left onto Maple Drive.
- Before registering for classes, be sure to see which courses are being offered.

Exception:

Then does not require a comma.

2. Use a comma after the first part of a compound sentence.

Examples:

- You should wash the rice for two to three minutes, and then you can start boiling the water.
- We played together as children, and ten years later we worked in the same company.
- I asked the older students which classes to take, and they recommended a few to me.

Exception:

In very short sentences, commas can be omitted.

- I sing and you dance.
- Turn right and walk ten minutes.

3. Use a comma to separate the items in a series. A series is three or more things. Things can be words or groups of words. Remember: No comma is used between a list of two things.

Examples:

- We have a cat, goldfish, and bird at our house.
- Every morning, I get up at seven, take a shower, eat breakfast, read the news, check my email, and study English.
- Before registering for classes, make sure to read the course list, talk to older students, and make a study plan.

NOTE:

Some people use no comma between the last two items. In this course, use all the commas. It will make your meaning clearer.

Example:

- I have visited many countries in Asia, Europe, and Africa.

콤마 규칙 세가지

1. 먼저, 다음에, 그 후에, 할머니의 집에 가기 전에 등의 시간 순서를 나타내는 표현 뒤에 쉼표를 붙이십시오.

예:

- 첫째, 그릇에 쌀을 부으십시오.
- 그 후에, Maple Drive 쪽으로 좌회전하십시오.
- 수업에 등록하기 전에, 그 코스가 개설되어 있는지 확인하십시오

예외:

Then에는 쉼표가 필요하지 않습니다.

2. 중문의 첫 부분(절) 뒤에 쉼표를 사용하십시오.

예:

- 당신은 2~3분 정도 쌀을 씻어야 합니다, 그리고 나서 물이 끓이기 시작해야 합니다.
- 우리는 어렸을 때 함께 놀았습니다. 그리고 나서 10년 동안 우리는 같은 회사에 근무했습니다.
- 나는 선배들에게 어떤 수업을 들을 지에 대해 물었습니다, 그러자 그들은 저에게 몇 가지를 권장했습니다.

예외:

아주 짧은 문장에서는 쉼표를 생략할 수 있습니다.

- 나는 노래하고 당신은 춤을 춥니다.
- 우회전해서 10분 동안 걸으십시오.

3. 일련의 항목을 구분하기 위하여 쉼표를 사용하십시오. 시리즈란 세 가지 또는 그 이상의 것들을 말합니다. 단어들 또는 단어들의 그룹일 수 있습니다. 주의 사항: 콤마는 두 가지의 목록 사이에 사용되지 않습니다.

예:

- 우리는 집에서 고양이, 금붕어, 그리고 새를 키우고 있습니다.
- 매일 아침, 저는 7시에 일어나서, 샤워를 하고, 아침식사를 하고, 신문을 읽고, 이메일을 확인하고, 그리고 영어공부를 합니다.
- 수업을 등록하기 전에, 반드시 코스목록을 읽어야 하고, 선배들과 이야기를 하고, 학습계획을 만들어야 합니다.

참고:

일부 사람들은 마지막 두 항목 사이에 쉼표를 사용하지 않습니다. 이 수업에서는 쉼표를 모두 사용하십시오. 쉼표는 의미를 좀 더 명확하게 합니다.

예:

- 나는 아시아, 유럽 및 아프리카 여러 나라를 방문했습니다.

Task 4

다음 단락을 읽고 필요한 쉼표를 추가하십시오. 일부 문장은 쉼표가 필요하지 않습니다.

My Dad, the Music Fan

My Dad is a music fan. His favorite genres of music are ballads rock and hip hop. He listens to rock songs in the morning sings ballads in the afternoon and practices hip hop dancing in the evening. He also watches concerts and dance competitions on TV. Our living room looks a karaoke room and his bedroom looks like a dance studio. There are guitars drums microphones and CDs all around the house. Sometimes I wonder if my father is a businessman or a pop idol.

Task 5

다음 지시사항에 따라서 각 문장을 완성하고, 적절한 곳에 콤마를 넣으시오.

Example:

Write a sentence that lists three foods you like.

I like *Korean kimchi, Mexican tacos, and French croissants*.

Write a sentence that lists...

1. three subjects you have studied.

   I've studied ______________________________.

2. Three places you would like to go in the future.
   I'd like to go to ______________________________

3. Five useful items to take when traveling to a different city or country.
   When you travel to a different city or country, be sure to take ____________________.

4. Two hobbies you have.
   My hobbies are ___________________________.

5. Three things you do on the weekends.
   Every weekend, I ______________________________.

WRAP-UP

1. Time-order paragraphs
2. Planning a paragraph: Outlining
   - Brainstorm to get ideas
   - Edit the brainstorming list
   - Organize the list
3. Commas: Three rules

1. 시간순서에 따른 단락
2. 단락 계획하기: 개요 작성
   - 아이디어를 얻기 위한 브레인스토밍을 하라
   - 브레인스토밍한 목록을 수정하라
   - 목록을 조직화하라
3. 콤마: 세 개의 규칙

Unit 4

Living from Day to Day II

INTRODUCTION

Topic: Living from day to day
Writing Process: Editing a paragraph
Sentence Structure: Compound sentence, coordinating conjunctions
Grammar: Comma rules II

주제: 하루 하루 살아가기
쓰기: 단락 편집
문장구조: 중문, 등위접속사
문법과 구두점: 콤마 규칙 II

WRITING PROCESS

1. Unedited paragraph

My routine

I get up 7:30, and eat breakfast. Then, my mom drives me to school. It takes about 30 minutes. It makes her exhausted. At school I study English math Korean science and other stuff. I like art music and P.E.

but math is too hard. I go home 3:00. My mom make some snack and then she helps my homework. At 6:00, I help my mom cook several dishes for dinner. After dinner I take a bath brush my teeth and put on my pajamas. Then, we watch TV together until bedtime. This is the most happy time of my day.

2. Edited paragraph

My routine → Center the title. (R)

Indent the first sentence.

I get up (at) 7:30, and eat breakfast. Then, my mom drives me to school. It takes about 30 minutes(, and it) makes her exhausted. At school I study English, math, Korean, science, and other stuff. I like art (and) music, ~~and P.E.~~ but math is too hard. I go home (at) 3:00. My mom make(s) some snack(s) and then she helps (me with) my homework. At 6:00, I help my mom cook several dishes for dinner. After dinner, I take a bath, brush my teeth, and put on my pajamas. Then, we watch TV together until bedtime. This is the ~~most happy~~ (happiest) time of my day.

3. Final paragraph

My Routine

I get up at 7:30 and eat breakfast. Then my mom drives me to school. It takes about 30 minutes, and it makes her exhausted. At school I study English, math, Korean, science, and other stuff. I like art and music, but math is too hard. I go home at 3:00. My mom makes some snacks, and then she helps me with my homework. At 6:00, I help my mom cook several dishes for dinner. After dinner, I take a bath, brush my teeth, and put on my pajamas. Then we watch TV together until bedtime. This is the happiest time of my day.

나의 일상

나는 7시 30분에 일어나서 아침식사를 합니다. 그러면 나의 어머니가 나를 학교까지 차로 데려다 주십니다. 약 30 분이 소요하는데, 이것이 그녀를 지치게 합니다. 나는 학교에서 영어, 수학, 국어, 과학 및 기타과목을 공부합니다. 나는 예술, 음악, 체육을 좋아하지만 수학은 너무 어렵습니다. 나는3시에 집으로 갑니다. 어머니께서 간식을 좀 만드시고 난 후 나의 숙제를 도와주십니다. 6시에, 나는 어머니가 저녁 식사를 위하여 요리하는 것을 돕습니다. 저녁 식사 후에 나는 목욕을 하고, 양치를 하고, 잠옷을 입습니다. 그리고 나면 우리는 취침 시간까지 함께 TV를 시청합니다. 이 시간은 나의 하루 중 가장 행복한 시간입니다.

Task 1 Editing awkward expressions

다음 단락을 읽고 밑줄 친 부분을 적절한 표현으로 바꾸어 쓰시오.

My Daily Routine

When I get up in the morning, the first thing I do is make some coffee (1) for helping me wake up. (2) During the coffee is brewing, I pour a bowl of frozen berries and wait for them to thaw. I usually eat breakfast (3) in the front my computer while checking my email. (4) After, I take a shower and fix my hair. Then I have to pick out my clothes for work, and I usually choose a comfortable (5) one piece. If I have plenty of time, I take the subway to work, (6) except I'm running late, I take a taxi instead. I work for 8 hours, and then I go back home. If I have energy, I will go for a run or ride my bike. Then I make dinner, study English (7) as possible I can, and go to bed.

(1) for helping → ______________________

(2) During → ______________________

(3) in the front my → ______________________

(4) After → ______________________

(5) one piece → ______________________

(6) except → ______________________

(7) as possible I can → ______________________

SENTENCE STRUCTURE

Compound sentences and coordinating conjunctions

1. Compound sentences

Compound means that there are 2 or more of something. A compound verb means that there are 2 or more verbs. A compound subject means that there are 2 or more subjects. A compound sentence means that there are two simple sentences joined together to form one sentence.

Simple Sentence + Simple Sentence = Compound Sentence

"My sister lives in Dallas." is a simple sentence.
"My brother lives in London." is also a simple sentence.

The two simple sentences can be joined together to form a compound sentence.

S+V, (connecting word) S+V
My sister lives in Dallas, and my brother lives in London.

When writing compound sentences you must remember these rules.
A compound sentence can be joined by one of two things:

a. A semi-colon ;
b. A comma and coordinating conjunction
*coordination conjunctions –and, but, or, for, yet, etc.

• Jaeho is a college graduate, but he can't find a job.

OR

• Jaeho is a college graduate; he can't find a job.

1. 중문

복합이란 2개 또는 그 이상의 것이 있다는 것을 의미합니다. 복합동사는 2개 또는 그 이상의 동사가 있는 것을 의미합니다. 복합주어는 2개 또는 그 이상의 주어가 있다는 것을 의미합니다. 중문이란 2개의 단문들이 하나의 문장의 형태로 합쳐지는 것을 의미합니다.

단문 + 단문 = 중문

주어와 동사, (연결어) 주어와 동사
"나의 여동생은 달라스에 삽니다"는 단문입니다.
"나의 남동생은 런던에 삽니다" 또한 단문입니다.

2개의 단문이 하나의 중문을 형성하기 위해 합쳐질 수 있습니다.
나의 여동생은 Dallas에 살고, 나의 남동생은 London에 삽니다.

중문을 쓸 때, 이러한 규칙들을 반드시 기억해야 합니다.
중문은 다음 2개중 하나의 방법에 의해 합쳐질 수 있습니다.

a. semi-colon (;) 을 쓰거나
b. 콤마와 and, but, or, for, yet 등의 등위접속사를 씁니다.

• 재호는 대학 졸업생이지만, 직장을 구하지 못한다.

2. Coordinate conjunctions: and, but, or, so

When you write compound sentences, you need to use coordinate conjunctions. The coordinate conjunctions have the following meanings.

(1) ***And*** connects two sentences with similar ideas; the sentences can be positive or negative.

- William washed the clothes, **and** Harry hung them out to dry.
- Hermione welcomed the guests at the door, **and** Ron led them to their seats.
- Artie wrote the lyrics to the song, **and** Brittany wrote the music.

(2) ***But*** connects two sentences with contrasting or opposite ideas.

- Sandra invited Myeong-soo to the party, **but** she didn't invite Ha-Ha.
- I usually don't eat dessert, **but** today I had some ice cream.
- I thought the show would be sold out, **but** actually nobody came.

(3) ***Or*** connects two sentences that express alternatives or choices.

- You had better pass the test, **or** you will fail the class.
- We can leave tonight, **or** we can leave early tomorrow morning.
- The bus might have arrived at 6:00, **or** it might have gotten here a bit earlier, **but** it definitely wasn't late.

(4) ***So*** connects a reason and a result

- I didn't use sunscreen, **so** my face got burned.
- Our teacher caught a cold, **so** she couldn't come to class.
- There was an accident on the highway, **so** the traffic was jammed.

2. 등위접속사: and, but, or, so

중문을 쓸 때는 등위접속사가 필요합니다. 등위접속사는 다음과 같은 뜻을 갈습니다.

1. 'and' 는 비슷한 아이디어를 가진 두 문장을 연결하는데, 이때 그 문장은 긍정문일 때도 있고 부정문일 때도 있습니다.

- William 옷을 세탁했고 Harry 는 그것들을 말리기 위해서 널었습니다.
- Hermione은 문에서 손님을 맞이했고 Ron은 그들을 자리로 안내했습니다.
- Artie는 작사를 했고 Brittany는 작곡을 했습니다.

2. 'but' 은 대조되거나 반대되는 아이디어를 연결합니다.

- Sandra는 파티에 명수는 초대했지만 하하는 초대하지 않았습니다.
- 난 보통 디저트를 먹지 않지만 오늘은 아이스크림을 먹었습니다.
- 나는 이 공연이 매진 될 것이라고 생각했지만 실제로는 아무도 오지 않았습니다.

3. 'or' 는 대안이나 선택을 표현하는 두 문장을 연결합니다.

- 당신은 이 테스트를 통과해야만 합니다. 그렇지 않으면 수업에서 낙제를 할 것입니다.
- 우리는 오늘 밤 떠날 수도 있고 내일 아침 일찍 떠날 수도 있습니다.
- 그 버스는 6 시에 도착했을 수도 있고 또는 조금 일찍 여기로 왔을 수도 있습니다. 하지만, 확실히 늦지는 않았습니다.

4. 'so' 는 이유와 결과를 연결합니다.

- 나는 자외선차단제를 사용하지 않았습니다. 그래서 내 얼굴이 탔습니다.
- 우리 선생님은 감기 걸렸습니다, 그래서 그녀는 수업에 올 수 없었습니다.
- 고속도로에서 사고가 있었습니다. 그래서 교통체증이 있었습니다.

Task 2 Classifying sentences

다음 각 문장을 읽고, 단문은 'S.'로 중문은 'C'에 표시하시오.

	S	C
1. Yesterday I cleaned my room and walked the dog.	_____	_____
2. Tonight we want to see a movie, but we don't know which one to watch.	_____	_____
3. My brother and I are very close.	_____	_____
4. She went shopping but forgot to buy eggs and vegetables.	_____	_____
5. It's raining today, so we can't do the laundry.	_____	_____
6. My teacher and his family don't like mushrooms or shellfish.	_____	_____
7. After dinner we can go to a musical or sing karaoke.	_____	_____

Task 3 Making compound sentences

단문을 결합하여 중문을 만드시오.

Example:

My roommate likes classical music. She doesn't like rock.
→ My roommate likes classical music, but she doesn't like rock.

1. Hong-cheol brought the cake. Jae-seok brought the ice cream.
→ ____________________

2. G-Dragon and T.O.P. had a fight. The concert was cancelled.
→ ____________________

3. Soo-young is tall. Sunny is short.
→ ____________________

4. I was late to class. My teacher punished me.
→ ____________________

5. Last night Dad made dinner. Last night Mom washed the dishes.
→ ____________________

6. We have to hurry. We will be late for the train.
→ ____________________

7. I wanted to wake up early this morning. I forgot to set my alarm.
→ ____________________

GRAMMAR

Comma rules II

Commas: four more rules

1. To separate every three digits in big numbers

- The world population surpassed the 7,000,000,000 mark in the year 2011.
- More than 5,000,000 people pass through that station every week.

cf) But NOT in years or street address numbers, or in decimals, or to separate dollars from cents

- the year 1999 (not 1,999)
- 1910 Washington Avenue (not 1,910 Washington Avenue)
- $39.99 (not $39,99 – in the U.S.)
- seven and three quarters = 7.75 (not 7,75)
- 3,456 thousandths of a meter = 0.3456 m (not 0.3,456 m)

2. To separate the month and day from the year when writing a date

- The PRC was formally established on October 1, 1949.

3. To separate street from city and city from state in a mailing address

- Fill out your application and send it to Columbia University at the following address: 1116 Amsterdam Avenue, New York, NY 10027.

4. (1) After the greeting in a personal letter (but not a business letter)

- Dear Dad,
- Dear Aunt Judy,
- To Whom It May Concern: (not To Whom It May Concern,)

(2) After the closing in personal letters and business letters

- Love, (personal)
- Sincerely,
- Yours sincerely,
- Respectfully yours,
- Faithfully yours

콤마: 다른 4가지 규칙

1. 큰 숫자를 각각 3개의 숫자 단위로 나눌 때 사용합니다.

- 2011년 세계인구가 70억 명을 넘어섰습니다.
- 500백만 이상의 사람들이 매주 저 역을 통과합니다.

연도, 거리 주소번호, 소수점 또는 센트에서 달러를 분리할 때는 사용하지 않습니다.

- 1999년
- 1910 Washington Avenue
- 3달러 99센트
- 7.75
- 0.3456 미터

2. 날짜를 쓸 때 연도에서 달과 요일을 구분할 때 사용합니다.

- PRC는 1949년 10월 1일에 공식적으로 설립되었습니다.

3. 우편주소에서 도시로부터 길 이름 그리고 주로부터 도시를 분리할 때 사용합니다.

   • 신청서를 완성하셔서 다음 주소의 콜롬비아 대학으로 보내시오: 1116 Amsterdam Avenue, New York, NY 10027.

4. (1) 개인적인 편지에서 인사말 다음에 사용합니다. (비즈니스 편지에서는 사용하지 않습니다.)

   • 아빠에게,
   • Judy 이모에게,
   • 관계자 분께,

   (2) 개인적인 편지나 비즈니스 편지에서 끝맺음 말 후에 사용합니다.

   • 사랑하는
   • 진심으로,
   • 진심으로,
   • 존경을 담아,
   • 신의를 표하며

Task 4

위에 소개된 규칙에 따라서 다음 문장에 콤마를 쓰시오.

1. Barack Obama resides at 1600 Pennsylvania Avenue Washington D.C.
2. The World Trade Center in New York was attacked on September 11 2011.
3. More than 700000000 species of animal life have been found in that region alone.

4. Last year, her annual salary was increased from $59560.50 to $61345.
5. The percentage of change amounted to exactly 0.28456 degrees.
6. Dear Mr. Gates I am writing to offer a business proposition...
7. Dear Grandma Thank you so much for the birthday gift...

Task 5

지금까지 배운 모든 콤마 규칙에 따라서 다음 문장에 콤마를 쓰시오.

1. Her parents live in Los Angeles California but they have a small vacation home in Boulder Colorado.
2. According to my friend's uncle aliens visited Earth 250000 years ago.
3. Please note that all letters sent to our office at 17 Fulton Street Brooklyn will be forwarded to the main headquarters at 1800 Seventh Avenue Manhattan.
4. Olivia woke up took a shower got dressed and went to school.
5. Because my mother works so hard during the day she never has any energy in the evening.
6. I fell asleep during the exam yesterday but nobody woke me up.
7. New York is predicted to have over 9000000 people by the year 2015.

WRAP-UP

1. Editing a paragraph
2. Compound sentences
3. Coordinating conjunctions: and, but, or, so
4. Four more comma rules

1. 단락 수정하기
2. 중문
3. 등위접속사: and, but, or, so
4. 네 개의 다른 콤마 규칙

Unit 5

The World around Us I

INTRODUCTION

Topic: The world around us
Writing Process: Space-order paragraphs
Grammar: Adjectives, prepositions, and prepositional phrases

주제: 우리들 주변 세상
작문: 공간 순서에 따른 단락
문법: 형용사와 전치사

OUR LIFE

Setting: The lounge of Super Duper English Academy
Characters: Katherine, Fred
Topic: The World Around Us

Fred : Good morning, Katherine.
Kathy : Hey, Fred. How was your weekend?
Fred : Oh, it was really fun! I did a homestay in Gyeongi-do, at

Minho's house.

Kathy : No way, really? How was it?

Fred : It was awesome, but I think I messed up a few times.

Kathy : How so?

Fred : Well, when I first walked in through the front door, Minho's little brother and sister starting shouting and pointing at my feet.

Kathy : Oh, Fred. Did you forget to take your shoes off?

Fred : Yup, you guessed it. But how was I supposed to know? We never take our shoes off when we enter a house in America.

Kathy : Well, things are a little different here. Did everything else work out okay?

Fred : No, that was just the beginning. After we got inside, I went to put some stuff in the fridge, just like Minho asked me to. But his mother was like, "No, no, no!" She took all the stuff out of that fridge and put it into another one. I had no idea what was going on.

Kathy : Ah, you probably put the stuff into the kimchi fridge by mistake.

Fred : The kimchi fridge?

Kathy : Yeah. Most families in Korea have two refrigerators – one for kimchi, and one for everything else.

Fred : Ah…it all makes sense now! Anyway, enough about me… how was your weekend?

Kathy : Oh, it was great! I managed to finish my plans for "the perfect vacation!"

Fred : The perfect vacation? Cool! Where are you planning to go?

Kathy : I'll tell you all about it at lunch. We'd better hurry or we'll be late for class.

Fred : OK, let's go!

Translation

배경 : Super Duper 영어 아카데미 라운지

인물 : Katherine, Fred

Fred : 좋은 아침이야, Katherine

Kathy: 응, Fred. 주말 어떻게 보냈니?

Fred : 정말 재미있었어! 경기도에 있는 민호네 집에서 홈스테이 했어

Kathy: 말도 안돼, 정말? 어땠어?

Fred : 굉장했어, 근데 실수도 몇 번 했어.

Kathy: 어떻게?

Fred : 음, 내가 처음 현관으로 들어갈 때, 민호의 동생들이 소리를 지르면 내 발을 가리켰어.

Kathy: 그랬구나, Fred. 신발 벗는걸 잊었었니?

Fred : 응, 맞췄네. 근데 내가 그걸 어떻게 알았겠어? 미국에서 집에 들어갈 때는 우리는 신발을 벗지 않고 들어가거든.

Kathy: 그러게, 여기는 좀 달라. 다른 건 다 괜찮았니?

Fred : 아니, 그건 아주 시작에 불과했어. 우리가 집에 들어갔을 때, 민호가 부탁해서 내가 냉장고에 뭘 넣으러 갔었거든. 그런데 민호 어머니가 "안돼, 안돼, 안돼!"라고 말하시는 것 같았어. 어머니는 그 냉장고에서 다시 꺼내셔서 다른 냉장고에 넣으시지 뭐니. 그 상황이 이해가 잘 안됐어.

Kathy: 아! 네가 실수로 김치 냉장고에 넣었나 보네.

Fred : 김치냉장고?

Kathy: 응 한국에서는 대부분 냉장고가 두 개야 –김치 냉장고랑 일반 냉장고가 있어.

Fred : 그렇구나...... 이제 이해가 되네! 어쨌든 내 얘기는 이 정도로 하고 넌 주말 어떻게 보냈니?

Kathy: 응, 아주 좋았어! "완벽한 휴가" 계획을 다 세울 수 있었지!

Fred : 완벽한 휴가? 멋지다! 어디로 갈 계획이야?

Kathy: 점심시간에 다 말해줄게. 우리 서둘러 가지 않으면 수업에 늦겠어.

Fred : 응, 가자!!

Words & expressions

① no way	말도 안돼
② awesome	경탄할만한, 엄청난
③ mess up	엉망이 되다, 실수를 하다
④ How so?	그래서? 어떻게?
⑤ yup/nope	YES/NO
⑥ How was I supposed to know?	내가 어떻게 그걸 알았겠어요?
⑦ work out okay	잘 풀리다
⑧ just the beginning	단지 시작
⑨ have no idea	전혀 모르겠다
⑩ make sense	말이 되다
⑪ anyway	어쨌든
⑫ enough about me…	간신히 어떤 일을 해내다
⑬ manage to do sth.	그것에 관해 다 이야기하다

Comprehension questions

1. What did Fred do over the weekend?
   (1) He stayed at home.
   (2) He made kimchi.
   (3) He went to Minho's house.
   (4) He had a "dream vacation."

2. What did Fred forget to do when he entered Minho's house?
   (1) keep his shoes on
   (2) remove his shoes
   (3) buy the kimchi
   (4) put the kimchi in the fridge

3. What are Katherine and Fred planning to discuss at lunch?
   (1) Katherine's vacation
   (2) Fred's vacation
   (3) Katherine's homestay
   (4) Fred's homestay

WRITING PROCESS

Space-order paragraphs

You will now learn to write good descriptions.

- To describe a person, you tell what the person looks like.
- To describe a place, you tell what it looks like.
- To describe a scene with people, you might first describe the place and then describe the people.
- To write a good description, use space order and specific details.

Space-order paragraphs

1. Describing from top to bottom

For example, when you describe a person, you might start by describing the person's head. You might work your way down the person's body and end at the person's feet. (hair→face→torso and arms→hips and legs→feet)

In this picture:

- The man has very short brown hair.
- He has a young face.
- He is wearing a green shirt and watch on his left wrist.
- He is wearing blue jeans.
- He has on black canvas shoes.

2. Describing from left to right

You might describe a room from left to right. For example, imagine you are standing at the doorway to your kitchen. You describe the things you see from the left side to the directly across from you to the right side. (left side→far side→right side)

In the picture below:

- On the left side, there are two ovens built into the wall.
- On the far side, there are cupboards and drawers, a stovetop, fan, pot, and pan.
- On the right side, there is a sink and faucet.

3. Other ways to describe a place

- bottom to top
- right to left
- far to near; near to far
- outside to inside; inside to outside

이제부터는 묘사를 잘하는 법을 배우게 될 것입니다.

- 사람을 설명할 때는, 그 사람이 어떻게 생겼는지를 묘사한다.
- 장소를 설명할 때는, 그 장소가 어떻게 보이는지를 묘사한다.
- 사람과 풍경을 설명할 때에는, 장소를 먼저 그 다음으로 사람을 묘사한다.
- 좋은 설명을 위해서는, 공간 순서와 구체적인 점들을 사용하여 묘사한다.

공간 순서에 따른 단락

1. 위에서 아래로 묘사하기

예를 들어, 사람을 묘사할 때, 머리부터 묘사하여 시작해 나가면 됩니다. 그 다음 몸, 그리고 나선 마지막으로 발을 묘사하면 됩니다. (머리→얼굴 →몸통과 팔→엉덩이와 다리→발)

이 그림을 보면,

- 그 남자는 아주 짧은 갈색 머리를 가지고 있습니다.
- 그는 동안입니다.
- 그는 초록색 셔츠를 입고 있고 왼쪽 손목에 시계를 차고 있습니다.
- 그는 청바지를 입고 있습니다.
- 그는 검정색 캔버스화를 신고 있어요.

2. 왼쪽에서 오른쪽으로 묘사하기

하나의 방을 왼쪽에서 오른쪽으로 묘사할 수 있습니다. 예를 들면, 부엌 문 쪽에 당신이 서 있다고 상상해 보십시오. 당신이 서 있는 곳 기준으로 왼쪽에서 당신 바로 건너편, 그리고 오른쪽으로 묘사해 보십시오. (왼쪽→ 건너편 쪽→오른쪽)

아래 그림을 보면,

- 왼쪽에, 벽에 장착된 두 개의 오븐이 있습니다.
- 건너편 쪽에, 찬장과 서랍, 스토브, 팬, 냄비, 그리고 프라이팬이 있습니다.
- 오른쪽으로는, 싱크대와 수도가 있습니다.

3. 다른 순서로 공간 묘사하기

- 아래에서 위로
- 오른쪽에서 왼쪽으로
- 먼 곳에서 가까운 곳으로; 가까이에서 먼 곳으로
- 밖에서 안으로; 안에서 밖으로

Task 1 Outline for a space-order paragraph

다음은 한 거실 사진입니다. 그 속의 가구들을 살펴봅시다. Word Bank에 있는 단어를 이용하여 왼쪽부터 쭉 방에 있는 모든 물건들을 차례로 나열해 보시오.

Word Bank:

window
sofa and cushions
TV
fireplace
sliding door 1
coffee table
armrest chair and cushions
sliding door 2

1.________

2.________

3.________

4.________

5.________

6.________

7.________

8.________

Task 2 Describe a scene

다음 그림을 보고 아래 질문에 답해보시오

1. Where is this scene taking place?
   a. At a beach
   b. At a park
   c. In someone's garden
   d. None of the above

2. Which of the following does NOT describe the people in the scene?
   a. A family taking a walk
   b. A couple sitting on the bench
   c. A man riding his bicycle
   d. Dogs running on the path

3. Which of the following best describes this scene?
   a. The sun is setting over the park. There are many animals in the lake.
   b. It is crowded on Sundays at the park. There is a family taking a walk, while a man rides his bicycle. Three joggers pass a couple sitting on a bench, staring at the mountains.
   c. There is a man riding a bicycle in the park. There are families and joggers too. Also a couple is sitting on a bench. There is a park.
   d. None of the above.

Task 3 Describing a person

다음 사진에 있는 소녀를 위에서 아래로 묘사해 보세요. 정답은 다양하게 나올 수 있습니다.

GRAMMAR

Adjectives & prepositions

1. Adjectives

Adjectives describe nouns and pronouns. Adjectives tell us what people (or things) look like, what kind they are, or how many of them there are.

what kind?	gentle cat, scary movie
which one(s)?	fifth grade, other people
how many or how much?	three tickets, most player

(1) Many adjectives come in front of nouns.

- a few colorful tropical birds
- four young Chinese high school students
- many crazy purple-haired girls
- sixteen large brown buildings

(2) Adjectives can follow linking verbs.

- The smell of the onion was strong.
- The price seems high.
- The girl looks beautiful in blue.
- He felt happy when he heard the final results.

(3) Adjectives are always singular.

• a seven-foot wall	(not a seven-feet wall)
• a ten-dollar bill	(not a ten-dollars bill)
• a five-year-old child	(not a five-years-old child)

(4) *–ing* and *–ed* words can be adjectives.

- a jogging suit
- the boring class
- the sleeping baby
- the broken chair
- the bored students
- the stolen jewelry

형용사와 전치사

1. 형용사

형용사는 명사와 대명사를 묘사해 줍니다. 형용사는 사람(또는 사물)이) 어떻게 보이는지, 어떤 종류인지, 얼마나 많은지를 우리에게 알려줍니다.

어떤 종류?	얌전한 고양이, 공포 영화
어떤 것(들)?	5학년, 다른 사람들
얼마나 많이?	세 개의 티켓, 대부분의 선수들

(1) 대부분의 형용사는 명사 앞에 위치합니다.

- 몇몇 다채로운 열대 새들
- 네 명의 어린 중국 고등학생들
- 많은 제정신이 아닌 듯한 보라색 머리를 한 소녀들
- 16개의 큰 갈색 빌딩들

(2) 형용사는 연결 동사 다음에 오기도 합니다.

- 그 양파 냄새가 강했습니다.
- 가격이 비싼 것 같습니다.
- 파란색 옷을 입고 있는 그 소녀는 예뻐 보입니다.
- 그는 최종 결과를 들었을 때 기뻤습니다.

(3) 형용사는 항상 단수형으로 쓰입니다.

- 7 피트의 벽
- 10 달러 지폐
- 5살 된 아기

(4) *-ing* 와 *-ed* 단어들도 형용사로 쓰입니다.

- 운동복 부서진 의자
- 지루한 수업 지루해진 학생들
- 자고 있는 아기 도난 당한 보석

2. Prepositions

Prepositions are little words such as ***in, of, at, from, behind, during, after, until, across***. Some prepositions are made of two words (e.g., ***according to, because of, out of, next to***) or even three words (e.g., ***in front of, in spite of, in addition to***).

about	between	past
above	beyond	since
across	by	through
after	down	throughout
against	during	till
along	except	to
among	for	toward
around	from	under
at	in	underneath
before	into	until
behind	like	up
below	of	upon
beneath	on	with
beside	over	without

※ Some compound prepositions:

according to	in place of
aside from	in spite of
because of	next to
in addition to	on account of
in front of	out of

2. 전치사

전치사는 as *in, of, at, from, behind, during, after, until, across*와 같은 짧은 단어들입니다. 두 개의 단어로 이루어진 것도 있고 (예를 들면, *according to, because of, out of, next to*), 세 개의 단어로 이루어진 것도 있습니다. (예를 들면, *in front of, in spite of, in addition to*).

하나의 단어로 이루어진 전치사

about ~에 대한	between 사이에	past 지나서
above ~보다 위에	beyond ~너머	since ~부터(이후)
across 건너서	by ~옆에	through ~통해
after ~뒤에(후에)	down 아래에	throughout 도처에, ~동안 죽
against ~에 반대하여	during ~동안	till ~까지
along ~을 따라	except 제외하고는	to ~로, ~쪽으로
among ~가운데	for ~위한	toward ~쪽으로
around 주위에	from ~에서(부터)	under ~아래에
at ~에(서)	in ~에(서), 안에	underneath ~밑에
before ~전에	into ~안으로	until ~까지
behind ~뒤에	like ~와 비슷한	up 위에
below 아래에	of ~의	upon = on
beneath 아래에	on ~위에	with ~와 함께
beside 옆에	over ~위에	without ~없이

※ 복합 전치사

according to ~에 따르면
aside from ~외 에는
because of ~때문에
in addition to ~에 더하여
in front of ~의 앞쪽에
in place of ~대신에
in spite of ~에도(불구하고)
next to ~바로 옆에
on account of ~때문에 (해서)
out of ~바깥에

3. Prepositional phrases

Prepositions are usually combined with a noun or noun phrases to makc a prcpositional phrasc such as *at school* or *behind the garage*.

(1) Prepositional phrases of place

- at school
- on the table
- next to the door
- in front of the theater
- between the University of Wisconsin and Carroll College

(2) Prepositional phrases of time

- at noon
- before class
- in the afternoon
- in 2012
- on that unforgettable October night

(3) Prepositional phrases that show possession

- (the mother) of the bride

- (the inside) of my desk
- (the owner) of the company
- (the pile) of dry leaves

(4) Other prepositional phrases

- (the woman) in the dark blue dress
- (the teacher) from Belgium
- (the man) with a fishing pole
- (a small house) with cracks in the walls

3. 전치사구

전치사는 대개 명사나 명사구와 결합하여 *at school, behind the garage*와 같이 하나의 새로운 전치사구를 만듭니다.

(1) 장소에 관한 전치사 구

- 수업 중
- 탁자 위에
- 문 옆에
- 극장 앞에서
- University of Wisconsin과 Carroll College 사이에

(2) 시간에 관한 전치사 구

- 정오에
- 수업 전에
- 오후에
- 2012년에
- 잊을 수 없는 10월의 저녁에

(3) 소유를 나타내는 전치사 구

- 신부의 (어머니)

• 책상 (안)
• 회사의 (소유자)
• 말라버린 잎 (더미)

(4) 기타 전치사 구

• 짙은 푸른색 드레스를 입고 있는 (여자)
• 벨기에 출신의 (선생님)
• 낚싯대를 들고 있는 (남자)
• 벽에 금이 가 있는 (작은 집)

Task 4

다음의 단락을 읽고, 굵게 표시되어 있는 명사들을 묘사하는데 쓰인 형용사들을 다 나열해 보시오.

Example:

The last **meal** I ate was expensive and delicious.
meal: last, expensive, delicious

My First Apartment

My first **apartment** was small, dark, and ugly. It was a cramped, two-room flat in a dirty old **building** in Brooklyn. The tiny **kitchen** was greasy and disgusting, and the smelly **bathroom** was always wet and covered in mold. The worst was the rat-infested living room. It was filled with stinky used **furniture**, and was always dusty no matter how much I tried to clean it. My favorite spot in the apartment was the little pink **bedroom**. The windowless **room** was quiet and boring but at the same time, peaceful and relaxing. I guess it doesn't sound so great, but it was my home, and I loved it.

1. apartment: ______________________________
2. building: ______________________________
3. kitchen: ______________________________
4. bathroom: ______________________________
5. furniture: ______________________________
6. bedroom: ______________________________
7. room: ______________________________

Task 5

아래 단락에서, 모든 전치사구에 밑줄을 치고, 각각의 전치사에 다음과 같이 표시를 하시오.

Example:

The tallest building (in) the world is (in) Dubai.

My Car

The outside of my car is always clean and shiny, but the inside of my car is always a mess. On the driver's seat there is a lot of pocket change, and in the passenger's seat are many magazines. Receipts are scattered across the dashboard, while the floor of the front seat is filled with trash. That sounds bad, but the area behind the front seats is even worse! The only tidy spot in the back is the baby seat. Next to the baby seat is a huge teddy bear named Edward, and the space between Edward and the door is completely stuffed with toys of all shapes and sizes. I have absolutely no idea what is beneath the seats. Sometimes I think it might be easier to buy a new car than to clean this one!

WRAP-UP

1. Space-order paragraphs
   - Describing from top to bottom
   - Describing from left to right
2. Adjectives
3. Prepositions,
4. Prepositional phrases

1. 공간순서를 나타내는 단락
   - 위에서 아래로 묘사하기
   - 왼쪽에서 오른쪽으로 묘사하기
2. 형용사
3. 전치사
4. 전치사구

Unit 6

The World around Us II

INTRODUCTION

Topic: The world around us
Writing Process: Editing a paragraph
Sentence Structure: Prepositional phrases in space and time order
Grammar: Result clauses (*so~that, such~that*)

주제: 우리 주변 세계
쓰기: 단락 수정하기
구조: 공간과 시간 순서를 표현하는 전치사구
문법: 결과를 표현하는 절 (*so~that, such~that*)

WRITING PROCESS

1. Unedited paragraph

The Perfect Vacation Spot

I went to Waikiki about fifteen years ago. I still have good memories about that trip until now, and I want to go at vacation on Hawaii again. The scenery in the island is fantastic, and the weather is great.

In the nearby Waikiki there are many interested shopping malls, delicious restaurants, and beautiful beaches. Even though the weather is always hot, I didn't feel so hot indoor the hotel because of the low humidity. Hawaiians are optimistic and friendly, so I felt relaxing whenever I saw them. If you are interested in the perfect vacation, I strongly recommend Hawaii to you. You will never feel boring there.

2. Edited paragraph

The Perfect Vacation Spot ——→ **Center the title.**

Indent the first sentence.

I went to Waikiki about fifteen years ago. I still have good memories about that trip until now, and I want to go ~~at~~ **on** vacation ~~on~~ **to** Hawaii again. The scenery ~~in~~ **around** the island is fantastic, and the weather is great. ~~In the nearby~~ **Near** Waikiki there are many ~~interested~~ **interesting** shopping malls, delicious restaurants, and beautiful beaches. Even though the weather is always hot, I didn't feel so hot ~~indoor~~ **inside** the hotel because of the low humidity. Hawaiians are optimistic and friendly, so I felt ~~relaxing~~ **relaxed** whenever I saw them. If you are interested in the perfect vacation, I strongly recommend Hawaii to you. You will never feel ~~boring~~ **bored** there.

3. Final paragraph

The Perfect Vacation Spot

I went to Waikiki about fifteen years ago. I still have good memories about that trip, and I want to go on vacation to Hawaii again. The scenery around the island is fantastic, and the weather is great. Near Waikiki there are many interesting shopping malls, delicious restaurants, and beautiful beaches. Even though the weather is always hot, I didn't feel so hot inside the hotel because of the low humidity. Hawaiians are optimistic and friendly, so I felt relaxed whenever I saw them. If you are interested in the perfect vacation, I strongly recommend Hawaii to you. You will never feel bored there.

완벽한 휴가지

나는 15년 전 와이키키 해변에 갔습니다. 난 지금도 그 여행에 있어서 좋은 기억을 가지고 있고 다시 하와이로 휴가를 떠가고 싶습니다. 그 섬 주변풍경이 너무 멋지고 날씨도 좋습니다. 와이키키해변 근처에는 많은 쇼핑몰들, 맛있는 레스토랑과 아름다운 해변들이 있습니다. 비록 날씨는 항상 더웠지만, 습도가 낮았기 때문에 호텔 내부에서는 그리 덥게 느껴지진 않았습니다. 하와이인들은 긍정적이고 친절해서, 그들을 볼 때마다 마음이 편했습니다. 완벽한 휴가를 원한다면, 당신에게 하와이를 강력하게 추천하고자 한다. 거기에서는 결코 지루해지지 않을 겁니다.

Task 1 Editing awkward expressions

다음의 단락을 읽고 밑줄 친 단어들을 적절하게 바꾸시오.

The Perfect Vacation Spot

I (1) have ever been to Hawaii about fifteen years ago, so I still have good memories about that trip. I want to go on vacation to Hawaii again. I will get a hotel room (2) which I can see the beach. There are palm trees, clean air, and fresh water. It is warm and a bit hot in (3) a day time, but it doesn't feel so hot in the house because of (4) the little humid, and it is cool at night. People (5) which lives there look bright and kind. They are easygoing and relaxed, so it feels great to meet them.

(1) have ever been → ______________________

(2) which → ______________________

(3) a day time → ______________________

(4) the little humid → ______________________

(5) which lives → ______________________

SENTENCE STRUCTURE

Prepositional phrases in space and time order

Prepositional phrases of time and place can be in different places in a sentence. Changing the location of a prepositional phrase can make a sentence more interesting. Stay away from always using the subject-verb-object pattern, so your writing style is more engaging.

Usual Pattern: The view from the living room window is especially beautiful in the fall.

New Pattern: In the fall, the view from the living room window is especially beautiful.

Or: From the living room window, the view is especially beautiful in the fall.

Translation:

Tip 1: You can move a prepositional phrase in a sentence that contains "there is" or "there are".

Usual Pattern: There is a large lake next to the park.

New Pattern: Next to the park, there is a large lake.

Tip 2: Notice that a comma is placed after a prepositional phrase that comes at the beginning of a sentence.

*Sometimes a prepositional phrase of place and subject can exchange places when the sentence only contains a subject(s), a verb, and a prepositional phrase. Here, there's no need for a comma.

S
Usual Pattern: The Matterhorn rose proudly in the background.
S
New Pattern: In the background rose the Matterhorn.

Tip 3: Only prepositional phrases that tell a time or a location can be moved.

I can't remember the name of your teacher.

Not Possible: Of your teacher, I can't remember the name.
The man in the black suit is a world-famous wrestler.
Not Possible: In the black suit, the man is a world-famous wrestler.
Possible (time): In the summer, the weather is hot and humid in Korea.
Possible (location): In Korea, the weather is hot and humid in the summer.

공간과 시간순서를 표현하는 전치사구

시간과 장소에 관한 전치사 구는 한 문장에서 서로 다른 위치에서 사용될 수 있습니다. 전치사구의 위치를 바꾸는 것은 문장을 더욱 흥미롭게 만들 수 있습니다. 항상 정해진 주어-동사-목적어 패턴을 바꾸어서 작문 스타일을 더욱 멋지게 만들어보세요.

기본 패턴: 거실 창문에서 보이는 풍경은 가을에 특히 아름답습니다.
새로운 패턴: 가을에는, 거실 창문에서 바라본 풍경이 특히 아름답습니다.
혹은: 거실 창문에서 보면, 그 풍경이 가을에 특히 아름답습니다.

팁1. 전치사구를 "there is" 혹은 "there are" 가 포함된 문장 속에서 옮길 수 있습니다.

기본 패턴: 공원 옆에는 큰 호수가 있습니다.
새로운 패턴: 공원 옆에 큰 호수가 있습니다.

팁2. 문 두에 오는 전치사구 뒤에는 콤마가 온다는 것을 유념하세요.

*문장이 주어, 동사, 전치사 구를 포함하고 있을 때, 때때로 장소를 나타내는 전치사구와 주어의 자리가 바뀔 수 있습니다. 여기에서는 콤마를 쓸 필요가 없습니다.

기본 패턴: 마터호른이 배경에 당당하게 솟아 있었습니다.
새로운 패턴: 배경에 마터호른이 당당하게 솟아 있었습니다.

팁3. 오직 시간과 장소에 관한 전치사구만 자리를 이동할 수 있다.

나는 당신의 선생님 성함을 기억하지 못합니다.

검정색 정장을 입은 그 사람은 세계적으로 유명한 레슬링 선수입니다.
여름에 한국에서는 날씨가 덥고 습합니다.
한국에서는 여름에 날씨가 덥고 습합니다.

Task 2

각 문장에서 전치사 구를 찾아 그 아래에 쓰시오.

1. In the center of the yard is a fountain.

   ____

2. Water splashes from the fountain onto some rocks around it.

   ________________, ________________

3. Under the trees there are wooden benches and tables.

____

4. Near the fountain stands a group of tall redwood trees.

____

5. After lunch it becomes very quiet in the cafeteria.

_______________, _______________

Task 3

먼저 각각의 문장을 읽고 전치사구에 밑줄을 치시오. 그리고 각각의 문장을 다시 쓰면서 시간이나 장소를 나타내는 전치사 구를 문두로 옮기고 필요시 콤마를 넣으시오.

Example:

There is a perfect place to take a vacation in Hawaii.
UNDERLINE: There is a perfect place to take a vacation <u>in Hawaii</u>.
REWRITE: <u>In Hawaii, there is a perfect place to spend a vacation</u>.

1. The Waikiki Sunrise Hotel is next to the beach.
UNDERLINE: The Waikiki Sunrise Hotel is next to the beach.
REWRITE: ______________________________

2. Four rooms are inside each suite: a master bedroom, a bathroom, a living room, and an entertainment room.
UNDERLINE: Four rooms are inside each suite: a master bedroom, a bathroom, a living room, and an entertainment room.
REWRITE: ______________________________

3. There is a luxurious Jacuzzi in every bathroom.

UNDERLINE: There is a luxurious Jacuzzi in every bathroom.

REWRITE: ____

4. A beautiful, sunny veranda is outside every living room.

UNDERLINE: A beautiful, sunny veranda is outside every living room.

REWRITE: ____

5. There are restaurants, cafes, and luxury boutiques on the first floor of the hotel.

UNDERLINE: There are restaurants, cafes, and luxury boutiques on the first floor of the hotel.

REWRITE: ____

6. The hotel staff will escort you to your room upon your arrival.

UNDERLINE: The hotel staff will escort you to your room upon your arrival.

REWRITE: ____

7. You will be treated like kings and queens until your departure.

UNDERLINE: You will be treated like kings and queens until your departure.

REWRITE: ____

Task 4

주어진 우리말 뜻에 맞도록 밑줄 친 곳에 적절한 전치사구를 써서 영어 문장을 완성하시오.

1. 리무진이 공항 밖에서 당신을 기다리고 있을 것입니다.
   → The limousine will be waiting for you ________________.

2. 우리는 폭포 위로 펼쳐지는 아름다운 무지개를 보았습니다.
   → We saw a beautiful rainbow ____________________.

3. 기내에서 담배를 피우시면 안됩니다.
   → You are not allowed to smoke ____________________.

4. 식료품점은 우체국과 은행 사이에 있습니다.
   → The grocery store is located ______________________.

5. 그 건물 주위에 경호원들이 있어서 우리는 하수구(sewer)를 통해서 도망쳐야 했습니다.
   → Since there were guards all ________________, they had to escape ________________.

6. 나는 그녀가 모자를 의자 밑에 두었다고 생각했는데, 침대 밑에 두었을 수도 있습니다.
   → I thought she left her hat ________________, but it might be ________________.

7. 당신의 컴퓨터를 가방에서 꺼내서 상자 안에 놓으시오.
   → Please take your laptop ____________________ and place it ____________________.

GRAMMAR

Result clauses (so…that; such…that)

We sometimes show cause and effect with the expressions *such* + noun + *that* or so + adjective/adverb + *that*.

such + noun + *that*

- It is such a lovely day that I don't want to go to work.
- He was such a handsome man that she couldn't look him directly in the face.
- She wrote such great songs that her popularity spread like wildfire.

so + adjective/adverb + *that*

- I am so hungry that I could eat a horse.
- The classroom was so quiet that you could hear a pin drop.
- He spoke so clearly that we could hear his every word.
- She had changed so much that I could hardly recognize her.

cf) *so that~can*

- She swims every day so that she can stay healthy.
- I stepped aside so that they could pass.

결과를 표현하는 절 (so…that; such…that)

우리는 때때로 such + 명사+ that 또는 so + 형용사/부사 + that의 표현들로 원인과 결과를 표현한다.

such + 명사 + *that* (너무 ~해서 ~하다)

- 날씨가 너무 좋아서 나는 일하러 가고 싶지 않습니다.
- 그는 너무 잘 생겨서 그녀는 그의 얼굴을 똑바로 쳐다보지 못했습니다.
- 그녀가 대단한 노래를 만들었기에 그녀의 명성은 삽시간에 퍼졌습니다.

so + 형용사/부사+ *that* (너무 ~해서 ~하다)

- 나는 너무 배가 고파서 말 한 마리도 먹을 수 있을 정도였습니다.
- 교실이 너무 조용해서 당신이 핀 떨어지는 소리도 들릴 정도였습니다.
- 그는 매우 분명하게 말을 해서 우리는 그의 모든 말을 알아들을 수 있었습니다.
- 그녀는 너무 많이 변해서 나는 그녀를 거의 알아 볼 수가 없었습니다.

cf) *so that~can* (하기 위해서)

- 그녀는 건강을 유지하기 위해서 매일 수영을 합니다.
- 나는 그들이 지나갈 수 있도록 옆으로 비켜섰습니다.

Task 5

왼쪽과 오른쪽에 있는 것을 서로 맞게 연결시켜 보시오.

A	B
(1) The weather is so hot...	(a) ...that you could get lost in it.
(2) It was such a difficult test...	(b) ...I wanted to crawl into a hole and die.
(3) The house is so huge...	(c) ...that I decided to drop the class.
(4) I was so embarrassed	(d) ...that we fell on the floor laughing.
(5) It was such a funny joke...	(e) ...that I feel like I am melting.
(6) I ate so much food...	(f) ...that my stomach is about to explode.
(7) Brad did such a terrible thing...	(g) ...that Angelina finally dumped him.

Task 6

다음의 주제를 가지고 "so…that"과 "such…that"을 넣어서 문장을 만들어 보시오.

(1) Your favorite place
(2) A movie you have seen
(3) A person you really like (or hate)
(4) A class/course you have taken

WRAP-UP

1. Editing a paragraph
2. Prepositional phrases in space and time order
   - Moving a prepositional phrase in a sentence
3. Result clauses: *so~that, such~that*

1. 단락 수정하기
2. 장소와 시간 순서를 표현하는 전치사구
   - 문장 안에서 전치사구 옮기기
3. 결과를 나타내는 절: *so~that, such~that*

Unit 7

Review

Unit 1

Introducing Ourselves and Others I

1. What is a paragraph?
2. How do you format a paragraph?
3. What does the writing process look like?
   - Prewriting: Brainstorming and outlining
     Writing the first draft
     Editing the first draft
     Writing the final draft
4. Sentences and fragments

1. 단락은 무엇인가
2. 단락은 어떻게 작성하는가?
3. 쓰기 과정은 어떠한가?
   - 쓰기 전 과정: 브레인스토밍과 개요
     초안 쓰기
     초안 편집하기
     최종 원고 쓰기
4. 문장과 문장의 일부

Task 1

아래의 박스 안에 있는 단어나 표현을 선택하여 빈칸을 채우시오. 필요하면 단어의 형태를 알맞게 바꾸시오.

retire	pass away	exhausted	get
I mean	figure	freshen up	be adopted
retire	let me guess		

1. I hope that my father __________ soon. He's getting old and I want to spend more time with him.
2. My mother works hard all day so she always feels __________ when she gets home.
3. You eat at MacDonald's every day? __________, you are American, right?
4. She __________ that I __________ because I don't resemble my parents at all.
5. I've been on the bus all day so I would like to _________ before we go out to eat.

Task 2

문장을 읽고 빈 칸을 채우시오.

How do you format a paragraph?

There are some IMPORTANT rules to remember when writing a paragraph.

(1) Give your paragraph a (________).
(2) (____) the first sentence of your paragraph about 1.25 cm in.
(3) (_________) each sentence at the end of the sentence that comes before it. (_____) each new sentence on a new line.
(4) (________) the whole word on the next writing line if a word is too long to fit at the end of a line.

Task 3

다음 주제를 읽고 밑줄 친 곳에 알맞은 문장을 써보시오.

TOPIC: Competitive Swimming, an Ideal Sport for Kids

Introduction

Competitive swimming provides same benefits as other sports
a. It is good exercise and builds muscular strength.
b. ____

Competitive swimming provides some additional benefits
a. Swimming is an important skill that can be used forever
b. ____
c. ____

My personal experience as a competitive swimmer
a. ____
b. ____

Conclusion

Task 4

아래의 단어의 그룹들을 읽고 그것이 문장이라면 S를 문장이 아니면 F에 표시하시오.

	S	F
1. Yes, I love.	_____	_____
2. My mother ate.	_____	_____
3. So excellent!	_____	_____
4. All of the students.	_____	_____
5. Listen!	_____	_____
6. My favorite aunt who is in Busan.	_____	_____

Unit 2

Introducing Ourselves and Others II

1. Editing a paragraph: My new teacher
2. Simple sentences
3. Connecting words: *and, but, or*
4. Punctuation: a period, a question mark, an exclamation point
5. Capitalization

1. 단락 수정: 나의 새 선생님
2. 단문
3. 연결어: and, but, or
4. 구두점: 마침표, 물음표, 느낌표
5. 대문자 사용

Task 5

다음 단락을 읽고 밑줄 친 부분을 적절한 표현으로 바꾸시오.

Oh, (1) I am so pool! When I (2) went to work every day, I am always late. This looks very bad and my boss (3) makes criticism. This makes me lose confidence in (4) oneself, thus I feel terrible at work. Then, after (5) I go to home and get stressed out that I may lose my job. This is not the only thing that troubles me, but it is the biggest.

(1) I am so poor! → ____________________!
(2) went to work → ____________________
(3) makes criticism → ____________________
(4) oneself → ____________________
(5) go to home → ____________________

Task 6

알맞은 접속사를 사용하여 다음 각 문장을 완성하시오.

1. Swimming __________ sailing are my favorite summer activities.
2. She likes her job, __________ hates her boss.
3. He has class on Mondays, Wednesdays, __________ Fridays.
4. They don't like beef __________ chicken.
5. My parents are very old __________ still energetic.
6. He can't play tennis, ride a horse, __________ skate very well.

Task 7

각 문장을 읽고 알맞은 구두점(마침표, 물음표, 느낌표)을 문장 끝에 넣으시오.

1. Isn't that the wrong answer __________.
2. I've never been to France __________
3. What I am trying to say is that I love you __________
4. Look out, there's a car coming __________
5. She's not late again, is she __________

Task 8 Capitalization

다음 단락을 읽고 대문자로 써야 할 부분을 고쳐 쓰시오.

Yesterday I watched an american tv show called fringe. it is about a special fbi team that investigates strange things in the world. I like the main character olivia, but I think the old scientist is a little strange.

Unit 3

Living from Day to Day I

1. Time-order paragraphs
2. Planning a paragraph: Outlining
   - Step 1: Brainstorm to Get Ideas
   - Step 2: Edit the Brainstorming List
   - Step 3: Organize the List
3. Three comma rules
   - After time-order expressions
   - After the first part of a compound sentence
   - To separate the items in a series

1. 시간순서에 따라 쓰는 단락
2. 단락쓰기 계획: 개요
   - 1단계: 아이디어를 얻을 수 있는 브레인스토밍
   - 2단계: 브레인스토밍한 목록 수정하기
   - 3단계: 목록을 구조화하기
3. 세 개의 콤마 규칙
   - 시간 순서를 나타내는 표현 다음에
   - 중문에서 첫 번째 절 다음에
   - 연속적으로 나오는 항목을 구별하기 위해서

Task 9

아래의 박스 안에 있는 단어나 표현을 선택하여 빈칸을 채우시오. 문맥에 따라 단어의 형태를 알맞게 바꾸시오.

grab	head	settle	stuff
give...a try	sticky	pretty much	kind of

1. If you're ready, let's __________ to the movie theater now.
2. There is so much __________ on my desk that I can't find the tickets.
3. I am __________ finished with the project, so we can leave soon.
4. Action movies can be __________ interesting sometimes, but I really prefer love stories.
5. Shall we __________ some popcorn before the film start?

Task 10 Brainstorming a list

학교에 가서 주로 하는 것들에 대해서 리스트를 작성해 보십시오. 예를 들어, 목록에 다음과 같은 것들을 넣을 수 있습니다.

- go to class
- review homework
- listen to lecture

순서에 신경쓰지 말고 아래에 모든 아이디어를 써보시오.

THINGS I DO WHEN I GO TO SCHOOL

____

____

____

____

____

____

Task 11 Revising your list

아래 박스 안에서 학교에서 하지 않는 일 세 가지를 고르시오.

a. go to class
b. review homework
c. have lunch with peers
d. watch the latest Hollywood movie
e. study at the library
f. attend seminars
g. eat at a fine dining restaurant
h. purchase new pets
i. walk around campus
j. go to the department office
k. attend lectures
l. go to events
m. read on the lawn

________, ________, ________

Task 12 Adding commas

다음 단락을 읽고 필요한 곳에 쉼표를 넣으시오. 어떤 문장은 쉼표가 필요하지 않습니다.

When James was a young man he used to love sports. Although he liked all kinds of physical activity, his favorite sports were baseball hockey and basketball. He played baseball in the spring and summer hockey in the winter and basketball all year round.

Unit 4

Living from Day to Day II

1. Editing a paragraph: My daily routine
2. Compound sentences: Simple Sentence + (connecting word) + Simple Sentence
3. Coordinating conjunctions: *and, but, or, so*
4. Four more comma rule
   - To separate every three digits in big numbers
   - To separate the month and day from the year when writing a date
   - To separate street from city, and city from state in a mailing address
   - After the greeting in a personal letter, and after the closing in personal and business letters

1. 단락 수정하기: 나의 일상
2. 중문: 단문 + 연결어 + 단문
3. 등위접속사: : *and, but, or, so*
4. 추가적인 4개의 콤마 규칙
   - 큰 숫자를 세 개의 숫자 단위로 나눌 때
   - 날짜를 쓸 때 연도에서 달과 요일을 구별할 때
   - 주소에서 도시와 도로 명을 구별할 때, 그리고 주와 도시를 구별할 때
   - 사적인 편지에서 인사말 다음에, 그리고 사적인 편지와 비즈니스 편지에서 끝맺는 말 다음에

Task 13 Compound sentences

두 개의 단문을 결합하여 하나의 중문으로 만드시오.

1. Class begins at 3:00 sharp. The exam will start at 3:10.
   → Class begins at 3:00 sharp, ____________________.

2. You have to study hard. You will fail the test.
   → You have to study hard, ____________________.

3. My sister loves to travel. She doesn't like to fly.
   → My sister loves to travel, ____________________.

4. It rained yesterday. The picnic was cancelled.
   → It rained yesterday, ____________________.

5. I really wanted to see the game. It was sold out.
   → I really wanted to see the game, ____________________.

Task 14 Classifying sentences

각 문장을 읽고, 그 문장이 단문이면 S에, 중문이면 C에 표시하시오.

	S	C
1. Yesterday I made my bed and walked the dog.	____	____
2. We want to go see the fireworks, but we're not sure we'll make it on time.	____	____
3. Me and my sister are very close.	____	____
4. She went shopping but forgot to buy tomatoes and ham.	____	____
5. It's raining today, so we can't go to the outdoor picnic.	____	____

Task 15 Making sentences with lists and commas

아래 각 주제에 맞게 문장을 쓰고, 필요한 곳에 쉼표를 넣으시오.

Example:

three people you admire
→ Three people I admire are my mother, my father, and Steve Jobs.

1. two of your favorite foods

____

2. four movies you like

____

3. the three biggest cities in Korea

____

Unit 5

The World around Us I

1. Space-order paragraphs
   - Describing from top to bottom
   - Describing from left to right
   - Other ways to describe a place
2. Adjectives and prepositions
   - Adjectives
   - Prepositions: one-word prepositions, compound prepositions
   - Prepositional phrases: a preposition + a noun or noun phrase

1. 공간 순서에 따라 쓰는 단락
   - 위에서 아래로 묘사하기
   - 왼쪽에서 오른쪽으로 묘사하기
   - 다른 방법으로 장소 묘사하기
2. 형용사와 전치사
   - 형용사
   - 전치사: 한 단어 전치사, 복합 전치사
   - 전치사구: 전치사 + 명사 또는 명사구

Task 16

아래의 박스 안에 있는 단어나 표현을 선택하여 빈칸을 채우시오. 문맥에 따라 단어의 형태를 알맞게 바꾸시오.

mess up	make sense	work out	awesome
no way	anyway	be like	by mistake
manage	yup		

1. Last night Aliyah called me and she __________, "Justin's presentation was so bad!"
2. I can't believe you __________ the project. What's wrong with you?
3. It turns out that he brought the wrong file __________.
4. It's too bad it didn't __________ well. __________, better luck next time!
5. Your explanation __________, but I still don't think the plan will work.

Task 17 Outline for a space-order paragraph

아래의 사진은 누군가의 거실입니다. 거실에 있는 가구들을 살펴보십시오. Word bank에 있는 단어들을 이용하여 왼쪽부터 차례로 물건들의 이름을 쓰시오.

Word Bank:

Window
Sofa and cushions
Curtains
Coffee table
Lamp
Futon with a book and game
Rug
Picture

1. ________________ 5. ________________

2. ________________ 6. ________________

3. ________________ 7. ________________

4. ________________ 8. ________________

Task 18 Describe a scene

아래의 사진을 보면서 각 질문에 알맞은 답을 고르시오.

1. Where is this scene taking place?
   a. At a beach
   b. At a park
   c. At a garden in someone's home
   d. At a swimming pool

2. Which of the following does NOT describe the people in the scene?
   a. family taking a walk
   b. People sunbathing.
   c. A child playing in the waves.
   d. A dog in a hospital.

3. Which of the following best describes this scene?
   a. The sun is setting over the beach. There are many animals in the sand.
   b. It is crowded on Sundays at the beach. There are many families sunbathing and enjoying the shade under their umbrellas. Kids and adults swim and frolic in the ocean. Everyone loves to spend a day at the beach.
   c. There is a man riding a bicycle in the park. There are families and joggers too. Also a couple sits on a bench. There is a park.
   d. None of the above.

Task 19 Prepositional phrases

다음 단락에서 전치사구를 찾고 전치사에 동그라미 표시를 하시오.

I will never forget the classroom of my first school. At the front was a huge blackboard, and at the back was a big playing area. Our teacher always brought fresh flowers to the classroom and put them next to her desk. Inside her desk she kept lots of candy, and under the desk a big pair of fuzzy slippers. Desks were arranged across the room, and between the desks animal prints were painted in various colors on the floor. We always felt safe and happy in that room.

Unit 6

The World around Us II

1. Editing a paragraph: The perfect vacation spot
2. Prepositional phrases in space and time order
   - Position of prepositional phrases
3. Result Clauses (*so~that, such~that*)
   - such + noun + that
   - so + adjective/adverb + that

1. 단락 수정하기: 완벽한 휴가 장소
2. 공간과 시간 순서에 따라 쓰는 글에서 전치사구
   - 전치사구의 위치
3. 결과를 표현하는 절(*so~that, such~that*)
   - such + 명사 + that
   - so + 형용사/부사 + that

Task 20

각 문장에 전치사구를 찾아서 각 문장 아래에 쓰시오.

1. In the center of the field there is a baseball mound.

   ____

2. Water splashes from the waterfall onto the rocks beneath.

   ____

3. Under the stars there are people watching and children dancing.

____

4. Near the entrance stands tall a gated fence.

____

5. After dinner it becomes very quiet in the house.

_______________________, _______________________

Task 21

각 문장을 전치사구 위치를 바꾸어 다시 써 보고, 필요한 곳엔 쉼표를 넣으시오.

1. There is a great place to spend a getaway weekend in Hawaii.
   → ____.

2. There is a beautiful garden around each villa.
   → ____.

3. The hotel staff brings you to your villa upon your arrival.
   → ____.

4. A small, private pool is outside near the beach.
   → ____.

5. There is also a spacious balcony outside the patio.
   → ____.

Task 22

의미가 통하도록 왼쪽에 있는 표현과 오른쪽에 있는 표현을 연결시키시오.

1. It was so cold that...
2. It was such a small sign that...
3. The class was so boring that...
4. His eyes were so intense that...
5. It was such an embarrassing situation that...

a) ...we drove right past it.
b) ...I couldn't feel my fingers.
c) ...I want to forget all about it.
d) ...everyone fell asleep.
e) ...I couldn't look at him.

Task 23

다음 각 주제에 맞게 "*so···that*"과 "*such···that*"이 들어간 문장을 만드시오.

Example:

somebody in your family

My sister studies so hard that she has no time to eat.

My sister is such a good student that she has never failed an exam.

1. a book you have read
   → ______________________________.
   → ______________________________.
2. your hometown
   → ______________________________.
   → ______________________________.

Unit 8

Exploring Social Issues I

INTRODUCTION

Topic: Exploring social issues
Writing process: Listing-order paragraphs
Grammar: Adverbs

주제: 사회적 쟁점들을 탐구하기
쓰기: 나열 순서에 따라 쓰는 단락
문법: 부사

OUR LIFE

Setting: The teachers' lounge at Super Duper English.
Characters: Katherine, Fred

Katherine enters, and Fred looks depressed.

Kathy : Hey Fred, what's wrong?
Fred : Oh, hey Katherine. What's wrong? Ah…it's nothing.
Kathy : Come on, Fred, you can talk to me. Something's got you down?

Fred : Well, I'm just confused really. I went down to Andong over the weekend, so I thought it would be nice to bring a gift back for our boss, but she wouldn't accept it.

Kathy : Oh, that's totally normal. She was just being polite – you have to insist that she take it.

Fred : Yeah, that's what I thought, so I did insist. After going back and forth a few times she finally accepted it, reluctantly, but she also specifically instructed me not to bring her any more gifts in the future. It didn't seem like it was just manners – she looked really serious!

Kathy : Ah. Well, perhaps she felt that accepting a gift from you was too much of a burden.

Fred : A burden? Why? I was just trying to be nice.

Kathy : You might see it that way, but social relationships are a little different here.

Fred : How so? Isn't a gift a gift?

Kathy : How can I explain? It's like…by giving her the gift, you were somehow implying that you deserved something in return, some kind of special treatment, and that might not have been appropriate for the relationship you have with her right now.

Fred : Okay, that kind of makes sense, but my students bring me gifts all the time. Just this morning Minho brought me a can of coffee when he came to class.

Kathy : Let me guess…he was late, right?

Fred : Yeah, how did you know that?!

Kathy : That's pretty common. In this case it's different – Minho knew that he was doing something wrong by coming late, so the gift was a way of "balancing out the scales."

Fred : Balancing…? (*confused expression*)

Kathy : Don't worry, Fred. You'll catch on soon. Come on, let's go to class!

Translation

배경 : Super Duper 영어학원의 교사용 라운지

인물 : Katherine, Fred

Katherine이 들어오고 Fred는 낙담한 것 같아 보인다.

Kathy: 안녕, Fred, 무슨 일 있니?

Fred : 안녕, Katherine. 무슨 일? 아무 일도 아니야.

Kathy: 왜 그래, Fred. 내게 얘기해봐. 무슨 신경 쓰이는 일 있구나?

Fred : 음, 그냥 단지 매우 혼란스러워. 주말 동안 안동에 갔어. 그래서 우리 상사를 위해서 선물을 사오면 좋겠다고 생각했지. 그런데 그녀는 받지 않았어.

Kathy: 아, 그건 정말 평범한 일이야. 그녀는 단지 예의 바르게 행동했던 거야 - 네가 그녀가 그 선물을 받도록 권유해야 해.

Fred : 응, 그게 바로 내가 생각 했던 거야, 그래서 나도 권유를 했어. 몇 번 왔다갔다한 후에, 그녀가 끝내 마지못해 받기는 했지만, 특별히 나에게 앞으로는 더 이상의 어떤 선물도 가져오지 말아달라고 지시했어. 그냥 예의상으로 말한 것 같아 보이지는 않았어 - 정말 진지해 보였거든.

Kathy: 음, 아마도 그녀가 네게 선물을 받는 것이 큰 부담이라고 느꼈나 봐.

Fred : 부담? 왜? 그냥 잘 대해주려고 한 것일 뿐인데?

Kathy: 그렇게 생각할 수도 있지. 그러나 인간 관계라는 것이 여기에서는 좀 달라.

Fred : 어떻게 다른데? 선물은 그냥 선물 아닌가?

Kathy: 어떻게 설명하면 좋지? 그녀에게 선물을 줌으로써 어떤 것, 어떤 특별한 대우 같은 것을 보답으로 받을 자격이 있다는 것을 나타내는 것 같기도 하고, 그것이 지금 현재 너와 그녀의 사이에서 적절하지 않을 수도 있고.

Fred : 알았어. 일리가 있는 것 같기도 하네. 하지만 내 학생들은 늘 내게 선물

을 가져오는걸. 오늘 아침에도 민호가 수업에 들어오면서 커피 한 캔을 줬어.

Kathy: 음, 예상해보자면, 걔 오늘 늦었지, 맞지?

Fred : 응, 어떻게 알았어?

Kathy: 그건 꽤 흔한 일이야. 이런 경우는 좀 다르지, 민호는 자기가 늦게 오는 것이 잘못된 것이라는 것을 알았고, 그 선물은 일종의 비율의 균형을 잡는 방법으로 볼 수 있지.

Fred : 균형......? (*혼란스러운 표정*)

Kathy: 걱정 마, Fred. 너도 곧 이해하게 될 거야. 자, 어서 수업 가자!

Words & expressions

① depressed/confused	우울한/혼란스러운
② What's wrong?	무슨 일이니?
③ Come on (persuasive)	한번 해봐 (설득력 있는)
④ Something got you down?	신경 쓰이는 일 있니?
⑤ Just being polite	예의일 뿐이야
⑥ insist that + subjunctive form (mandative construction)	~에게.. 할 것을 요구하다/주장하다/고집하다
⑦ reluctantly	마지못해서, 꺼려하면서
⑧ specifically instruct	특별히 지시하다
⑨ manners	매너
⑩ It's like~	~인 것 같다
⑪ somehow V-ing	왠지 ~하다
⑫ some kind of N	일종의 ~같은
⑬ appropriate (social nuance)	적절한(사회적인 뉘앙스)
⑭ to make sense	일리가 있다
⑮ balance out the scales	비율의 균형을 잡다
⑯ catch on	이해하다

Comprehension questions

1. Why did Fred buy a gift for his boss?
   (1) To thank her for her help.
   (2) To get better treatment from her.
   (3) To apologize for a mistake.
   (4) To be friendly.

2. Which is NOT one of the explanations Katherine provides for the boss's behavior?
   (1) The boss was showing good manners.
   (2) The boss did not like the gift.
   (3) The boss felt pressured to behave differently.
   (4) The boss felt overburdened.

3. Why does Katherine think Minho brought the coffee for Fred?
   (1) To help Fred stay alert in class.
   (2) To make up for his tardiness.
   (3) To make sure he won't be late again.
   (4) To be nice.

WRITING PROCESS

Listing-order paragraphs

1. Listing-order paragraphs

You already learned how to write a paragraph using time order and space order. Now you will learn about listing order.

In a listing-order paragraph, divide each topic into separate points. Discuss the first completely, and then another, and then a third point, and so on. The order is up to you.

Example:

A nurse should have at least five characteristics. First, he or she must really like people because the job requires dealing with sick people who are sometimes unpleasant and demanding. Second, a nurse must be organized. A nurse has to remember to give out medications. Third, a nurse must be calm. The job can be very stressful and the best decisions are made when one is calm. Also, a calm nurse is better able to soothe a sick patient. In addition, nurses need to be physically fit because the job requires standing and walking all the time. Furthermore, a nurse must be intelligent and adept in order to keep up with the complex machinery used in hospitals today.

1. 나열 순서에 따라 쓰는 단락

시간과 공간의 순서를 이용하여 단락을 쓰는 법에 대해서는 이미 배웠습니다. 이제 단락의 나열 순서에 대해서 배우겠습니다.

나열 순서에 따라서 쓰는 단락에서는 각 주제를 개별적인 요점으로 나눕니다. 첫 번째 요점을 완벽히 토의한 후에, 다른 것, 그리고 나서 세 번째 요점으로 계속 토의해 나가면 됩니다. 각각의 요점에 대한 토의 순서는 당신이 결정하면 됩니다.

간호사는 적어도 다섯 가지의 특징을 가지고 있어야 합니다. 첫 번째, 그 또는 그녀는 반드시 사람들을 정말 좋아해야 합니다. 왜냐하면 그 일은 가끔 불쾌하고 요구가 많은 아픈 사람들을 다루어야 하는 것이 요구하기 때문입니다. 두 번째, 간호사는 체계적이어야 합니다. 간호사는 약을 나눠줘야 하는 것을 기억해야 하기 때문입니다. 세 번째, 간호사는 침착해야 합니다. 그 일을 하면서 스트레스를 많이 받을 수 있고, 침착해야만 가장 좋은 결정을 내릴 수 있습니다. 또한,

침착한 간호사는 아픈 환자를 더 잘 진정시킬 수 있습니다. 게다가, 간호사들은 신체적으로 건강해야 할 필요가 있는데, 이 직업은 계속해서 서있거나 걸어 다녀야 하기 때문입니다. 더 나아가, 간호사는 오늘날 병원에서 쓰이는 복잡한 기계들을 잘 다루기 위해서 똑똑해야 하고 빠르게 배울 수 있어야 합니다.

2. Listing-order transition signals

In the model paragraph the writer introduces each of the three qualities with a transition signal: *First of all, second, and third.* These transition signals are the same as time-order transitions, but they don't show order in this case. Here they are used to list the characteristics. Thus, we call them **listing-order transition signals.** *Also, in addition*, and *furthermore* are other listing transition signals.

Listing-order transition signals

First,...	Second,...	Third,...
Fourth,...	...also...	First of all,...
Also,...	In addition,...	Furthermore,...

Tip: You can place listing-order transition signals at the beginning of the sentence, and put a comma after them. Also may come at the end of a sentence with or without a comma, or in the middle without a comma.

Example:

- Also, they are good friends.
- They are good friends also.
- They are also good friends.

2. 연결어

예로 제시된 단락에서 저자는 세 개의 특징을 각각 설명하기 위해서 연결어(transition signal)를 사용합니다: 첫 번째, 두 번째, 그리고 세 번째. 이러한 연결어는 시간순서를 나타나는 연결어와 같지만 이번 경우에는 순서를 보여주지는 않습니다. 여기에서는 특성을 나열하기 위해서 연결어를 사용하였기 때문에 나열 순서 연결어라고 부를 수 있습니다. *Also, In addition, Furthermore*는 또 다른 나열 순서 연결어입니다.

나열 순서 연결어

First,…	Second,…	Third,…	Fourth,…
…also…	First of all,…	Also,…	In addition,…
Furthermore,…			

Tip: 문두에 나열순서 연결어를 쓸 수 있는데 그 때는 뒤에 콤마를 써주어야 합니다. *Also*의 경우, 문미에 콤마와 함께, 또는 콤마 없이 올 수도 있고, 문장 중간에 콤마 없이 쓰일 수도 있습니다.

예:

- 또한, 그들은 좋은 친구 입니다.
- 그들은 좋은 친구입니다 또한.
- 그들은 또한 좋은 친구입니다.

Task 1

다음 단락에서 나열 순서를 나타내는 연결어를 찾아서 표시하시오.

Dogs make the best pets for three reasons. First of all, dogs are very loyal. Once you earn a dog's trust, he will always be your companion.

Second, they are fun. You can take a dog for a walk, play fetch and even go for a swim. Also, they can play with younger children, providing fun for the whole family. Third, dogs are very protective. If you are ever worried about a burglar, a dog is sure to bark loud to alarm everyone. In addition, they can protect the blind in their everyday life.

Task 2

인간 지능 (human intelligence)에 관한 다음 단락을 읽으시오. 빈 칸에 나열 순서를 나타내는 적절한 연결어를 쓰시오.

There are many different types of intelligence. (1)______________, there is the mathematical-logical type. People who have a high amount of this type of intelligence usually grow up to be scientists or engineers. (2) ______________, there is the linguistic type. People with high linguistic intelligence are good at using language, so they often become novelists, reporters, or poets. Most people already know about these two types. There are (3) ______________ musical and spatial varieties of intelligence. While musical intelligence is of obvious benefit to musicians, singers and composers, spatial intelligence is helpful for people like artists, urban planners, and architects. (4) ______________, there is the bodily-kinesthetic type of intelligence, which is possessed to high degrees by dancers, athletes, police officers and fire fighters. The final two types of intelligence are interpersonal and intrapersonal, which are usually found in leaders, managers, and organizers. The bottom line is, there are many ways to be "smart."

Task 3

당신이 제일 좋아하는 종류의 요리를 생각해 보시오. 좋아하는 음식을 적어도 3개를 쓰고 그것들에 대해 당신이 좋아하는 부분을 설명하시오. 나열 순서 연결어를 적절하게 넣어서 단락을 완성하시오.

GRAMMAR

Adverbs

1. Adverbs

Adverbs modify a verb and tell more about an action.

How?	The ship sails slowly.
When?	He came home late.
Where?	Stay inside.

How often? She often drinks tea.

Adverbs also modify adjectives and other adverbs.

1) Adverbs modifying verbs:
- She drives quickly and recklessly.
- Do it well or not at all.
- He loves her passionately.

2) Adverbs modifying adjectives:
- The new coach is surprisingly fit.
- His handwriting is incredibly nice.
- Jim's dog was horribly ugly.

3) Adverbs modifying other adverbs:
- She worked extremely quickly.
- They lived together very happily.
- He was hurt almost fatally.

1. 부사

부사는 동사를 수식하고 행동에 관해서 더 설명해 줍니다.

어떻게?	그 배는 서서히 항해했습니다.
언제?	그는 집에 늦게 왔습니다.
어디에?	안에서 있으세요.
얼마나 자주?	그녀는 자주 차를 마십니다.

1) 동사를 수식하는 부사
- 그녀는 너무 빠르고 무모하게 운전을 합니다.
- 잘하지 않을 거라면 아예 하지를 마세요.

• 그는 그녀를 열정적으로 사랑합니다.

2) 형용사를 수식하는 부사 :
- 새로 온 코치는 놀라울 정도로 몸이 탄탄합니다.
- 그의 손 글씨는 믿을 수 없을 정도로 예쁩니다.
- Jim의 개는 끔찍하게도 못생겼습니다.

3) 다른 부사를 수식하는 부사 :
- 그녀는 매우 빨리 일을 했습니다.
- 그들은 매우 행복하게 함께 살아갔습니다.
- 그는 거의 치명상을 당했습니다.

2. Formation of adverbs

1) Many adverbs are formed from an adjectives + *-ly*
- successful → successfully
- slow → slowly
- happy → happily

2) A few *-ly* words are adjectives.
- lovely
- friendly
- lonely

3) Some adverbs have two forms that have different meanings
- hard / hardly
  - She works <u>hard</u> these days.
  - I can <u>hardly</u> believe it.
- High / highly
  - Throw it as <u>high</u> as you can.
  - She is <u>highly</u> respected.

- late / lately
  - I arrived late for the meeting.
  - I haven't seen her lately.

2. 부사의 형태

1) 많은 부사들은 형용사에 *-ly*를 붙여서 만들어 집니다.
   - 성공적인 → 성공적으로
   - 느린 → 느리게
   - 행복한 → 행복하게
2) 몇몇의 *-ly* 단어들은 형용사입니다.
   - 사랑스러운
   - 친숙한
   - 외로운
3) 어떤 부사는 다른 의미를 갖는 두 개의 형태를 취합니다.
   - hard / hardly
     - 그녀는 요즘 열심히 일합니다.
     - 나는 도저히 그것을 믿을 수가 없습니다.
   - high / highly
     - 가능한 한 높이 던지세요.
     - 그녀는 매우 존경 받고 있습니다.
   - late / lately
     - 나는 그 회의에 늦게 도착하였습니다.
     - 나는 최근에 그녀를 본 적이 없습니다.

Task 4

다음 단락을 읽으며 부사에 밑줄을 그으시오.

My husband and I get along well, but our personalities are completely different. He talks, walks, eats and drinks very slowly, but I do everything quickly. He wakes up early every day, but I love to sleep late. He is quite passionate about his job and works diligently, but I hate my job and do it unenthusiastically. His side of the bedroom is neat and tidy, but my half is so messy. He drives slowly and cautiously, but I don't have the patience for that, so he thinks I am a dangerous driver. But I think these things are not really important. We love each other deeply and never fight at all, so I think we will live happily ever after.

Task 5

다음 상자 안에서 알맞은 단어를 골라 각 문장의 빈칸을 채우시오.

noisy – noisily	impatient – impatiently
angry – angrily	reckless – recklessly
fearful – fearfully	happy – happily

1. My older brother is a __________ driver. He always drives _________, no matter how much we try to persuade him to slow down.

2. The hungry tourists listened __________ while the guide explained the long history of the building. One member of the tour group grew so __________ that he snuck off to the cafeteria.

3. The __________ protesters marched down the road toward the plaza. Then, as the police began to set up barricades, the crowd __________ shouted at the officers.

4. I will __________ grant a reward to the person who finds my lost dog. She's a big, __________ Labrador Retriever with black hair.

5. Last weekend there was a __________ party in the restaurant down the block. I couldn't get to sleep because people were talking and singing __________ all night.

WRAP-UP

1. Listing-order paragraphs
2. Listing-order transition signals
   - First, second, also, first of all, in addition, furthermore,……
3. Adverbs
   - Adverbs modifying verbs, adjectives, and other adverbs
4. Formation of adverbs
   - Adjectives + *-ly*
   - A few *-ly* adjectives
   - hard/hardly, high/highly, late/lately

1. 나열순서에 따라 단락 쓰기
2. 나열순서를 나타내는 연결어
    - First, second, also, first of all, in addition, furthermore,……
3. 부사
    - 동사, 형용사, 다른 부사들을 수식하는 부사들
4. 동사의 형태
    - 형용사 + *-ly*
    - 몇 개의 *–ly* 형용사들
    - hard/hardly, high/highly, late/lately

Unit 9

Exploring Social Issues II

INTRODUCTION

Topic: Exploring social issues
Writing Process: Editing a paragraph
Paragraph Structure: Topic sentence, supporting sentences, and concluding sentence
Grammar: Run-on sentences

주제: 사회적 쟁점들 탐구
쓰기: 단락 수정하기
문장구조: 주제 문장, 뒷받침 문장, 결론 문장
문법: 계속되는 문장

WRITING PROCESS

1. Unedited paragraph

An ideal husband

I like an understanding husband. Whatever I say, I hope he will always agree with me. I'd like he is also open minded, with a sense of humor and not talkative. If he were talk a lot, I would feel tired.

I hope he'll have a lot of money and has an ability of his work as much as whatever he gives that I want to buy. I want to get a comfortable life when I get older. He should put his family first. He must be grown up a good family and I think his parents also definitely kind. Finally, I want he is taller than me because I'm a bit taller than other women.

2. Edited paragraph

An Ideal Husband → **Center the title.**

Indent the first sentence.

I like an understanding husband. Whatever I say, I hope he will always agree with me. ~~I'd like he is also~~ **would also like him to be** open-minded, with a sense of humor and not talkative. If he ~~were~~ talk**ed** a lot, I would feel tired. I hope he'~~ll~~ **will** have a lot of money and ~~has an~~ **have the** ability ~~of his~~ **to** work ~~as much as whatever he gives that~~ **hard enough to afford the things** I want to buy. I want to ~~get~~ **have** a comfortable life when I get older. He should put his family first. He must ~~be grown up~~ **have been raised in** a good family and I think his parents **should** also definitely **be** kind. Finally, I ~~want~~ **hope** he is taller than me because I'm a bit taller than other women.

3. Final paragraph

An Ideal Husband

I would like an understanding husband. Whatever I say, I hope he will always agree with me. I would also like him to be open-minded, with a sense of humor and not talkative. If he talked a lot, I would feel tired. I hope he will have a lot of money and have the ability to work hard enough to afford the things I want to buy. I want to have a comfortable life when I get older. He should put his family first. He must have been raised in a good family and I think his parents should also definitely be kind. Finally, I hope he is taller than me because I'm a bit taller than other women.

이상적인 남편

나는 이해심이 많은 남편을 바랍니다. 내가 무엇을 얘기하든지, 그는 항상 나에게 동의해주기를 바랍니다. 나는 또한 유머감각을 가진 마음이 넓고 수다스럽지 않은 사람이 좋습니다. 만약 그가 말을 많이 한다면, 나는 피곤할겁니다. 나는 그가 부유하고 내가 사고 싶은 것들을 충분히 살 수 있게 해줄 만큼의 일을 할 능력을 가진 사람이기를 바랍니다. 나는 나이가 들어서 편안한 삶을 살길 바랍니다. 그는 그의 가족을 우선순위로 두어야 합니다. 그는 좋은 가정환경에서 자랐어야만 하며 그의 부모님 또한 무조건 친절해야 합니다. 마지막으로, 나는 내가 다른 여자들보다 키가 좀 크기 때문에, 그도 나보다 좀 더 키가 크길 바랍니다.

Task 1 Editing awkward expressions

다음 단락을 읽고 밑줄 친 곳의 단어들을 적절한 표현으로 고치세요.

An Ideal Husband

In the future I (1) hope have a devoted husband and (2) a harmony family. So my ideal husband is (3) thoughtfully man who has a healthy way of thinking. Also he should have a positive attitude about domestic duties, helping me with infant care and housework. In addition, he should have (4) hobbies and likes the same like me. That is my idea of the perfect husband, but can I really find him?

(1) hope have → ____________________!

(2) a harmony family → ____________________

(3) thoughtfully man → ____________________

(4) hobbies and likes the same like me → ____________________

PARAGRAPH STRUCTURE

Topic sentence, supporting sentence, and concluding sentence

1. Topic sentence

The most important part of a paragraph is the topic sentence. The topic sentence lets the reader know what the topic of the paragraph is going to be. It is usually the first sentence in a paragraph.

There are two parts to a topic sentence: a topic and a controlling idea. The topic tells the reader what the paragraph is about, while the controlling idea limits what the paragraph will say about the topic.

Topic / ***Controlling Idea***
Driving on freeways demands skill and alertness.

Topic / ***Controlling Idea***
Television commercials are annoying for several reasons.

Usually, the topic comes first in the topic sentence, while the controlling idea comes second. However, the order can be reversed.

Example:

Topic / ***Controlling Idea***
a. An ideal spouse has several qualities.

Controlling Idea / ***Topic***
b. There are several qualities of an ideal spouse.

1. 주제 문장

단락의 가장 중요한 부분은 주제문장 입니다. 주제문장은 독자가 이 단락의 요점이 무엇이 될지를 알려줍니다. 주로 단락의 첫 문장이 주제문장 입니다.

주제 문장에는 2가지 부분이 있습니다: 주제와 조절하는 아이디어입니다. 주제가 독자에게 그 단락이 무엇에 관한 것인지를 말해주는 반면에, 통제하는 아이디어는 그 단락이 그 주제에 대해서 무엇을 말할 지를 밝힙니다.

고속도로에서 운전하기 위해서는 기술과 민첩성이 필요합니다.
텔레비전 광고는 몇 가지 이유로 인해 짜증스럽습니다.

대체로, 주제 문장에서 주제가 먼저 오고 생각을 밝히는 부분이 다음으로 오게 됩니다. 그러나 순서는 바뀔 수 있습니다.

예:

- 이상적인 배우자는 몇 가지 자질을 가지고 있습니다.
- 이상적인 배우자의 몇 가지 자질이 있습니다.

2. Supporting sentences

Supporting sentences are the middle sentences in a paragraph. They support or provide evidence for the idea of the topic sentence. Supporting sentences can be written in a listing type of paragraph. Remember from the previous unit the section about listing order paragraphs and writing things in order.

A paragraph must follow the rule of **unity**. This means that each paragraph is one unit, so all sentences must be about the main idea.

In other words, all supporting sentences must be **relevant** to the main idea. Anything not directly related to the main idea would be considered **irrelevant**.

Example:

- If your paragraph is about the harmful effects of alcohol:
- *Many people drink alcohol because it relaxes them* is irrelevant.

Tip:

When writing a paragraph, make sure to keep all supporting sentences relevant to the main idea.

2. 뒷받침하는 문장

뒷받침하는 문장들은 단락의 중간에 오는 문장들입니다. 주제문장의 아이디어를 뒷받침하거나 증거를 제공합니다. 뒷받침하는 문장들은 문단에서 나열형식으로 쓸 수 있습니다. 지난 과에서의 나열순서 단락과 순서대로 쓰기 부분을 기억해보십시오.

단락은 통일성의 규칙을 따라야 합니다. 이는 각각의 단락이 하나의 구성단위이므로 모든 문장들은 그 주제에 대한 내용이어야 한다는 것입니다.

다시 말해서, 모든 뒷받침 문장들은 주제와 연관되어 있어야 합니다. 주제와 직접적으로 관련되지 않은 것은 무엇이든지 연관이 없는 것으로 여겨질 것입니다.

예:

- 술의 나쁜 영향에 대해서 쓰는 단락이라면:
- *많은 사람들은 술이 그들을 편안하게 해주기 때문에 술을 마십니다* 는 관련되지 않은 내용입니다.

팁:

단락을 작성할 때, 모든 뒷받침되는 문장들이 주제와 관련 있는 내용이 되어야 하는 것을 명심해야 합니다.

3. Concluding sentence

Paragraphs that are not part of a longer composition often have a concluding sentence at the end. A concluding sentence closes the paragraph so that the reader is not expecting anything more. It can also remind the reader of the main point by restating the topic in different words.

Examples:

- All year round, a beach is a great place to have fun.
- In short, there are many ways to be intelligent.
- In brief, nursing is a profession for people who are patient, kind, and strong.
- I never thought I would be a pet lover, but our Sami, has made me change my mind.

Tip:

You may use a conclusion transition signal to tell your reader that this is the end of the paragraph. Try to avoid the overused ***In conclusion*** and ***In summary.*** Here are some examples.

Conclusion signals

In short.....	In brief.....	Indeed.....
In sum......	To summarize......	Finally.....
Therefore.....	Overall.....	

3. 결론 문장

긴 작문의 일부가 아닌 단락은 종종 끝에 결론 문장을 가지고 있습니다. 결론 문장은 독자가 더 이상의 것을 기대하지 않도록 하기 위해 단락을 마무리 짓습니다. 또한 다른 말로 주제를 다시 언급해줌으로써 독자가 주제를 상기할 수 있도록 해줍니다.

예:

- 1년 내내, 해변은 즐거운 시간을 보내기에 좋은 장소입니다.
- 요약하자면, 똑똑해질 수 있는 다양한 방법들이 있습니다.
- 요약하자면, 간호는 인내심 있고, 착하며 건강한 사람들에게 맞는 직업입니다.
- 나는 내가 애완동물을 사랑하는 사람이 될 줄은 생각지도 못했었는데, 우리의 Sami때문에 생각이 바뀌었습니다.

팁:

결론 부분에서 독자들에게 이 것이 단락의 마지막이라는 것을 알려주기 위해 연결사를 사용할 수 있습니다. 그러나 'In conclusion'과 'In summary' 와 같이 과도하게 많이 쓰이는 것은 피하는 게 좋습니다. 여기 몇 가지 예가 있습니다.

결론을 나타내는 연결사

요컨대......	간단히......	정말로......
요컨대......	요약하면......	마침내......
그러므로......	전반적으로......	

Task 2

다음 질문을 읽고, 가장 알맞은 답을 고르시오.

1. Which of the following is the best example of a topic sentence?
   a. In summer, you can swim.
   b. Beaches are fun in summer and in winter.
   c. Also, on a clear winter night, it is fun to sit around a bonfire.
   d. If you don't like to swim, you can relax on the sand.

2. Look at this sentence:
   A good architect is both an artist and a mathematician.

   What is the topic?
   a. A good architect.
   b. An artist and a mathematician.

3. Look at this sentence:

Artistic talent and mathematical ability are two qualities of a good architect.

What is the controlling idea?

a. A good architect

b. Artistic talent and mathematical ability

4. A topic sentence tells the reader what they are going to read.

a. TRUE

b. FALSE

5. A controlling idea tells the reader what the paragraph will discuss the topic.

a. TRUE

b. FALSE

Task 3

각각의 단락에서, 주제와 직접적으로 관련이 없는 문장을 찾아내시오.

1.

Elderly People

Another problem facing a number of elderly people is living on a reduced income. When they retire, old people may receive a pension from their company or a benefit from the government. The amount of their monthly income is often significantly less than they received when they were fully employed. All of a sudden, retirees find that they can no longer continue the life style that they had become accustomed to, even if that life style was a modest one. Many find, after paying their monthly bills, that there is no money left for a movie or dinner out. Of course, sometimes they cannot go out because of their health. For some elderly people, the small amount of money they receive will not even cover their monthly bills. They realise with horror that electricity, a telephone, and good food are luxuries they can no longer afford.

1. Irrelevant sentence: ______________________________

____

2.

Gregory

by *Barbara Carter*

Gregory is my beautiful gray Persian cat. He walks with pride and grace, performing a dance of disdain as he slowly lifts and lowers each paw with the delicacy of a ballet dancer. His pride, however, does not extend to his appearance, for he spends most of his time indoors watching television and growing fat. His familiarity with cat food commercials has led him to reject generic brands of cat food in favor of only the most expensive brands. Gregory is as finicky about visitors as he is about what he eats, befriending some and repelling others. He may snuggle up against your ankle, begging to be petted, or he may imitate a skunk and stain your favorite trousers. Gregory does not do this to establish his territory, as many cat experts think, but to humiliate me because he is jealous of my friends. My sister also has a dog named Gregory. After my guests have fled, I look at the old fleabag snoozing and smiling to himself in front of the television set, and I have to forgive him for his obnoxious, but endearing, habits.

2. Irrelevant sentence: ______________________________

____

Task 4

각 질문을 읽고 답하시오.

1. 다음 단락의 결론문장으로 가장 알맞은 것을 고르시오.

Humans have known that earthworms have been vital to enriching Earth's rich soil all throughout history. Egyptian Queen Cleopatra called earthworms sacred. The Greek philosopher Aristotle said earthworms were the 'intestines' of the soil. In 1881 Charles Darwin stated, "It may be doubted whether there are many other creatures which have played so important a part in the history of the world."

a. Could Earth support mankind without the earthworm?
b. People throughout history have understood that earthworms are extremely important.
c. Charles Darwin was a scientist.
d. Aristotle was a Greek philosopher and scientist.

2. 다음 단락을 읽고, 결론문장을 만들어서 쓰시오.

The one day I spent in Morocco, Africa was the experience of a lifetime. When I finally reached Morocco and got off the bus, there were four little girls standing shoeless in the hot sun. After I swallowed my tears, I could not even try to picture this in America as it is not something you often see in the U.S. Meanwhile my tour guide instructed me not to give them money as it encouraged the children to beg; however, I was wearing four silver bracelets. As I walked over to the girls, their eyes watched my every move. Then I kneeled down to their level while I gave each girl a bracelet. They stood there gleaming at me, for they were pleased. I felt completely in disbelief that this tiny gesture could mean so much.

~Kayla Marie Anfinson 2005~

Concluding sentence: ________________________________

____

GRAMMAR

Run-on sentences

1. Run-on sentences

A run-on sentence is a common writing error. When students write two sentences together without punctuation or a conjunction, this is called a run-on sentence.

Repairing run-on sentences

(1) Put a period between the two sentences, making two separate sentences. You can alternatively use a semicolon if the two sentences are strongly related.

(2) Add a comma and a coordinating conjunction, making a compound sentence.

2. Examples of run-on sentences

(1)

Run-on sentence:

- My friend's daughter is desperate to pass her exam she spends hours studying every night.

Repair job:

- My friend's daughter is desperate to pass her exam. She spends hours studying every night.
- My friend's daughter is desperate to pass her exam; she spends hours studying every night.
- My friend's daughter is desperate to pass her exam, so she spends hours studying every night.

(2)

Run-on sentence:

- We helped our teacher clean up the classroom then we went home.

Repair job:

- We helped our teacher clean up the classroom. Then we went home.
- We helped our teacher clean up the classroom, and then we went home.

(3)

Run-on Sentence:

- Big dogs take up too much space they need a lot of food.

Repair Job:

- Big dogs take up too much space. Also (What's more / Furthermore / In addition / Moreover), they need a lot of food.
- Big dogs take up too much space, and they need a lot of food, too.

1. 계속되는 문장

계속되는 문장은 글쓰기에서 흔히 나타나는 실수 입니다. 학생들이 두 개의 문장을 구두점이나 접속사 없이 쓰게 되면, 이것을 계속되는 문장이라고 합니다.

2. 계속되는 문장 예시

(1) 두 문장 사이에 마침표를 찍어서 두 개의 분리된 문장으로 만듭니다. 두 문장이 긴밀하게 연결되어 있다면 세미콜론을 쓸 수도 있습니다.

(2) 콤마와 등위접속사를 넣어서 하나의 중문을 만듭니다.

계속되는 문장 예시1

- 내 친구의 딸은 간절히 시험에 통과하기를 바랍니다 그녀는 매일 밤 몇 시간 동안 공부를 합니다.

계속되는 문장 예시2

- 우리는 우리 선생님이 교실 청소하는 것을 돕고 그리고 나서 집에 갔습니다.

계속되는 문장 예시3

- 큰 개들은 너무 많은 공간을 차지하고 그들은 많은 음식을 필요로 합니다.

Task 5

다음 계속되는 문장을 고쳐서 올바른 문장으로 쓰시오.

1. Some people like cats some people like dogs I like turtles.

   → ______________________________

2. Kittens are soft and fuzzy they like to play and take naps they are cute.

   → ______________________________

3. Puppies are cute too puppies can't protect you.

   → ______________________________

4. Dogs are loyal friends they comfort you welcome you home after work and protect you.

   → ______________________________

5. Lions and tigers are good protectors they eat too much food.

   → ______________________________

6. Monkeys like to swing around they like to play they are a little stinky.

   → ______________________________

7. Turtles are peaceful and they are gentle and they are very wise they are the best pets.

   → ______________________________

Task 6

다음의 계속되는 문장들을 수정하고, 그 문장들을 사용하여 적절한 곳에 단어를 더하거나 변경하여 단락을 형성하시오.

1. Many people think that women are weaker than men they are actually superior to men in many ways.
2. In most countries women live longer than men they live healthier than men.
3. Women are better than men at doing stuff these things involve the five senses.
4. Women have a stronger sense of smell they have a stronger sense of taste they have better vision and hear better.
5. On average women are physically weaker than men they are mentally stronger than men.
6. Men are more violent than women they commit more crimes women are compassionate and forgiving.
7. Consider all of these points you cannot deny that women are better.

WRAP-UP

1. Editing a paragraph: An Ideal Husband
2. Topic sentence
   - Topic + controlling idea
3. Supporting sentences
   - Support the idea of the topic sentence
   - Be relevant to the main idea
4. Concluding sentence
   - Close the paragraph
   - Restate the topic
5. Run-on sentences
   - Incorrect punctuation or absence of conjunctions
6. Repairing run-on sentences
   - Put a period (or semicolon) between the two sentences, making two separate sentences.
   - Add a comma and coordinating conjunction, making a compound sentence.

1. 단락 수정하기
2. 주제 문장
   - 주제 + 통제하는 아이디어
3. 뒷받침하는 문장들
   - 주제 문장의 생각 뒷받침 하기
   - 주제와 연관성이 있어야 함
4. 결론 문장
   - 단락 마무리하기
   - 주제 재언급하기
5. 계속되는 문장들
   - 잘못된 구두점 또는 접속사의 부재

6. 계속되는 문장들 수정하기

- 두 문장들 사이에 점(또는 세미콜론) 넣어서 두 문장을 독립된 문장들로 만들기
- 콤마와 접속사를 더해 중문으로 만들기

Unit 10

Keeping in Touch with Family and Friends I

INTRODUCTION

Topic: Keeping in touch with family and friends
Writing Process: Reasons and examples
Grammar: Transitional signals with reasons and examples

주제: 가족과 친구들과 연락하기
쓰기: 이유와 예시
문법: 이유와 예시를 나타내는 연결어

OUR LIFE

Setting: The teachers' lounge at Super Duper English.
Characters: Katherine, Fred

Katherine enters with a big smile.

Kathy : Hi, Fred!
Fred : Wow, somebody's looking cheerful today! Did you win the lottery or something?
Kathy : Nope, I just got back from the travel agency, and I am super

psyched!

Fred : Oh yeah? Where are you going?

Kathy : As soon as the semester is over I am going to visit my family back home. I'm *so* looking forward to it.

Fred : When's the last time you went back to the States?

Kathy : Let's see…I guess…yeah, it's been about three years now.

Fred : No way! Really? Don't you miss your family sometimes? And your friends?

Kathy : Yeah, sure. But I keep in touch with everyone pretty regularly. I Skype with my parents like clockwork, once a week, and I call my friends all the time.

Fred : Ah, Skype is that live video chat thing, right? Everyone's been telling me to try it, but I'm kind of a technophobe. I don't even know how to text.

Kathy : You've got to be kidding. For real, you don't even use email?

Fred : Well, email – yeah. In this day and age email is pretty much inevitable, but my parents live up in the mountains without an internet connection, so it's not really an option. Besides, I like writing letters – you know, real letters, on paper?

Kathy : OK, Grandpa! Do you come to work by horse and buggy, too?

Fred : (*chuckling*) Call me old-fashioned, but there is nothing like the feel of a real letter. You can read it over and over. You can touch it, you can smell it, you can almost see the person's soul right there on the page.

Kathy : Wow, that's pretty intense! I know what you mean, letters are pretty nice. I just wish I had the time to write them.

Fred : Yeah, that *is* a problem. Oh, speaking of the time, we're late!

Translation

배경 : Super Duper English의 선생님 라운지

인물 : Katherine, Fred

Katherine이 밝은 미소를 지으며 들어온다.

Kathy: 안녕, Fred!

Fred : 와, 오늘 활기차 보이는데! 복권당첨이라도 된 거야?

Kathy: 아니, 방금 여행사에서 돌아왔는데, 정말 너무 신이나!

Fred : 정말? 어디 가는데?

Kathy: 학기가 끝나자마자 나는 내 고향으로 가족을 만나러 갈 거야. 난 정말 기다려져.

Fred : 마지막으로 미국에 갔던 때가 언제야?

Kathy: 음, 그러니까 한 3년 된 것 같아.

Fred : 말도 안돼! 정말? 가끔 가족들이 그립지 않니? 친구들도?

Kathy: 응, 물론이지. 그런데 나는 모든 사람들과 꽤 정기적으로 연락을 하면서 지내. 나는 부모님과 일주일에 한번 규칙적으로 스카이프를 하고 내 친구들과는 항상 통화해.

Fred : 스카이프는 화상채팅을 말하는 거지? 맞지? 다들 내게 한번 시도해보라고 하는데 나는 과학기술을 겁내는 성향이 있어서. 나는 어떻게 문자 메세지를 보내는지도 몰라.

Kathy: 말도 안돼. 정말로, 너 이메일도 안 쓴단 말이야?

Fred : 이메일 - 그래. 요즘 시대에 이메일은 필연적인 것이지만, 나의 부모님은 인터넷 연결이 되지 않는 산 위에 사셔서 그렇게 선택사항은 아니야. 게다가, 나는 편지쓰기를 좋아해- 너도 알잖아, 종이에 쓰는 진짜 편지 말이야.

Kathy: 알겠어요, 할아버지! 마차 타고 출근 하는 건 아니지?

Fred : (*킬킬 웃으며*) 구닥다리라고 불러, 그러나 진짜 편지 느낌 만한 게 없어. 여러 번 읽을 수 있고, 만질 수도 있고, 냄새를 맡을 수도 있고, 그 페이지에서 그 사람의 영혼까지도 거의 볼 수 있어.

Kathy: 와, 그거 꽤나 강한데! 네가 무슨 말을 하는지 알겠어, 편지는 꽤 좋은 것이지. 나는 단지 내가 편지를 쓸 수 있는 시간이 있길 바라는 마음이야.

Fred : 맞아, 바로 그게 문제야. 시간얘기가 나와서 말인데, 우리 늦었어!

Words & expressions

① ...or something	(구어) ......또는 뭔가
② super + ADJ (colloquial)	정말/매우 ~한 (구어체)
③ psyched (colloquial; means 'excited')	흥분되는 (구어체)
④ as soon as...	~하자마자
⑤ be looking forward to + NP/ V-ing	~하기를 고대한다.
⑥ the States	미국
⑦ keep in touch / get in touch / be in touch	~과 연락하면서 지내다
⑧ Skype	스카이프, 화상 채팅
⑨ like clockwork	정확히, 규칙적으로
⑩ technophobe (sb. who fears technology)	테크노포비아 (기술을 겁내는 사람)
⑪ text (verb/noun)	(동사) 문자메시지를 보내다, (명사) 문자메시지
⑫ You have got to / must be kidding (colloquial)	농담임이 분명하다 (구어체)
⑬ for real (very colloquial)	진짜로 (구어체)
⑭ In this day and age	요즘 시대에
⑮ pretty much (colloquial; means 'almost entirely')	꽤나 (구어체: 거의 대부분)
⑯ inevitable	피할 수 없는, 필연적인
⑰ not an option	선택사항이 아닌
⑱ OK, Grandpa!	오, 할아버지!(구시대적인 사람을 놀리는 말투)
⑲ horse and buggy	마차 (구식)
⑳ call me old-fashioned, but...	구식이라고 불러, 그렇지만...
㉑ There's nothing like...	~처럼 좋은 것은 없다.
㉒ intense	격렬한, 열렬한
㉓ wish + past form VP	~할 수 있으면 좋겠다.
㉔ speaking of + NP	~에 대해 말하자면

Comprehension questions

1. Which word best describes Katherine's emotion as she enters the lounge?
   (1) excited
   (2) upset
   (3) regretful
   (4) curious

2. How does Katherine usually contact her parents?
   (1) by email
   (2) by phone
   (3) through text messages
   (4) through Skype

3. Why doesn't Fred use Skype?
   (1) He has no time.
   (2) He's afraid to use it.
   (3) It is too expensive.
   (4) It is too convenient.

4. Why does Katherine call Fred "Grandpa?"
   (1) He is much older than her.
   (2) He has a big beard.
   (3) He is old-fashioned.
   (4) He is actually her grandfather.

5. What is NOT one of the reasons Fred likes "real" letters?
   (1) He can physically touch them.
   (2) He can appreciate their scent.
   (3) He feels closer to the writer's spirit.
   (4) It takes time to write them.

WRITING PROCESS

Reasons and examples

We will now learn how to give reasons and to use examples to support your reasons. Remember that every paragraph has a topic sentence and supporting sentences. Using reasons and specific examples will help strengthen your idea or argument.

Example

Northern California

Northern California is a fantastic place to go on a vacation for two reasons. First of all, Northern California has an amazing amount of state parks, as well as national parks where one can see spectacular flora and fauna. In Redwood State Park, for example, tourists are able to see Sequoia trees as old as fifteen-hundred years. On the coast, at JV Fitzgerald Marine Reserve, travelers can observe seals nesting, mating, and giving birth. Secondly, Northern California has some of the greatest mountains for hiking and climbing in the world. Take Mount Shasta for example, in Shasta-Trinity National Forest. Mt. Shasta is 14,179 Ft./4322 m. tall and has over 460 miles/740 Kilometers of hiking trails for all seasons. The Sierra Nevada Mountains in Yosemite Park are accessible by car and are breathtaking. Indeed, Northern California is a wonderful place to go if you like the wilderness.

In the example, when you write a topic sentence such as *Northern California is a fantastic place to visit*, you need to support it with **reasons**. It's important to explain *why* Northern California is a fantastic place to visit. The writer in this model paragraph gave two main reasons why tourists enjoy visiting Northern California.

1. It has an amazing amount of state parks, as well as national parks where one can see spectacular flora and fauna.
2. It has some of the greatest mountains for hiking and climbing in the world.

After you state your reasons, it is necessary to support them. A good way is to give **specific examples.** These can be names of people, places, or things. They can also be exact numbers of things or amounts of money. In the model paragraph the writer gives two supporting details for each reason.

근거와 예시

모든 문단은 주제와 주제를 뒷받침해주는 문장들로 이루어져 있습니다. 근거들과 구체적인 예들을 이용해서 당신의 생각과 주장을 뒷받침 할 수 있습니다.

예

북부 캘리포니아

북부 캘리포니아는 두 가지 이유에서 휴가 때 방문하기에 환상적인 곳입니다. 우선 첫 번째로, 북부 캘리포니아는 다양한 동식물들을 볼 수 있는 국립 공원들뿐만 아니라, 놀랄 만큼 많은 수의 주립공원들을 가지고 있습니다. 예를 들어, Redwood 주립공원에서, 방문객들은 1500년 가량 된 세쿼이아나무들을 볼 수 있습니다. 해변가의, JV Firzgerald 해양보호

구역에서, 여행자들은 물개들이 둥지를 틀고, 짝짓기를 하고, 출산하는 모습을 관찰할 수 있습니다. 둘째로, 북부 캘리포니아는 하이킹과 등산을 하기에 좋은 세계적으로 훌륭한 산들이 있습니다. Shasta-Trinity 국립 숲에 있는 Shasta산을 예로 들어 봅시다. Shasta산은 높이가 14,179피트/4322미터이고 460마일/740킬로미터가 넘는 사계절을 위한 하이킹 트레일이 있습니다. Yosemite 공원에 있는 Sierra Nevada 산은 자동차로 접근할 수 있고 숨이 막힐 정도로 아름답습니다. 당신이 야생을 좋아한다면 북부 캘리포니아는 가 보아야 할 정말 멋진 곳입니다.

예문에서, *북부 캘리포니아는 휴가 때 방문하기에 환상적인 곳입니다* , 와 같은 주제문장을 쓸 때, 이를 뒷받침하기 위한 이유들이 필요합니다. *왜* 북부 캘리포니아가 방문하기에 좋은 곳인지에 대해 설명하는 것이 중요합니다. 이 예문의 글쓴이는 왜 관광객들이 북부 캘리포니아를 방문하는 것을 즐기는지에 대한 두 가지 중요한 이유를 제시합니다.

1. 북부 캘리포니아는 다양한 동식물들을 볼 수 있는 국립 공원들뿐만 아니라, 놀랄 만큼 많은 수의 주립공원들을 가지고 있습니다.
2. 북부 캘리포니아에는 하이킹과 등산을 하기에 좋은 세계적으로 훌륭한 산들이 있습니다.

이유들을 제시한 이후에, 그 이유들을 뒷받침하는 것은 필수적입니다. 특정한 예시들을 제시하는 것은 좋은 방법입니다. 사람들, 장소, 혹은 물건들의 이름이 될 수도 있습니다. 또한 정확한 숫자나 금액이 될 수도 있습니다. 예문에서 글쓴이는 각각의 이유에 대해 두 개의 뒷받침 예시들을 제시합니다.

Task 1

주어진 단락을 읽고 개요(outline)를 완성하시오.

Northern California

Northern California is a fantastic place to go on a vacation for two reasons. First of all, Northern California has an amazing amount of state parks, as well as national parks where one can see spectacular flora and fauna. In Redwood State Park, for example, tourists are able to see Sequoia trees as old as fifteen-hundred years. On the coast, at JV Fitzgerald Marine Reserve, travelers can observe seals nesting, mating, and giving birth. Secondly, Northern California has some of the greatest mountains for hiking and climbing in the world. Take Mount Shasta for example, in Shasta-Trinity National Forest. Mt. Shasta is 14,179 Ft./4322 m. tall and has over 460 miles/740 Kilometers of hiking trails for all seasons. The Sierra Nevada Mountains in Yosemite Park are accessible by car and are breathtaking. Indeed, Northern California is a wonderful place to go if you like the wilderness.

____________________(Title)

Topic Sentence: ______________________________

Reason A: ______________________________

Example 1: ______________________________

Example 2: ______________________________

Reason B: ______________________________

Example 1: ______________________________

Example 2: ______________________________

Concluding Sentence: ______________________________

Task 2

다음 개요를 보고 각각의 근거에 대해 적어도 한가지의 특정한 예시를 생각해서 쓰시오.

Small cars are more economical than big cars. (Topic)

A. They don't use much gasoline (Reason)

1. A Honda Civic gets forty miles per gallon. (Example)
2. ______________________________ (Example)

B. Maintenance Costs are lower. (Reason)

1. Since cars are smaller, the parts are cheaper to fix. (Example)
2. ______________________________ (Example)

C. Insurance is cheaper. (Reason)

1. Smaller cars are cheaper to fix; Thus insurance is cheaper. (Example)
2. ______________________________ (Example)

You save money on gas, maintenance and insurance when you own a small car.

Task 3

당신이 왜 CUFS(Cyber Hankuk University of Foreign Studies)를 선택했는지 그 이유를 생각해보고, 주제문을 완성하시오. 그리고 단락 개요를 완성하시오.

CUFS (Title)

Topic Sentence: I chose to attend CUFS for these two reasons: ____________________

Reason A: ______________________________

Example 1: ______________________________

Example 2: ______________________________

Reason B: ______________________________

Example 1: ______________________________

Example 2: ______________________________

Concluding Sentence: ______________________________

GRAMMAR

1. Transitional signals with reasons

First of all, + CLAUSE / Second, + CLAUSE

- There are many reasons why Seoul is a great place to visit. First of all, it has some of the best museums and cultural attractions in the world. Second, the cuisine is absolutely fabulous.

The first reason is that + CLAUSE / The second reason is that + CLAUSE

- I respect my father for several reasons. The first reason is that he is a dedicated and diligent man. The second reason is that he always does his best to love and support our family.

The first is + NP / The second is + NP

- There are several advantages to joining the marketing team here at Big Money, Incorporated. The first is the energetic and supportive work atmosphere in the department. The second is the impressive benefits package offered to all employees.

1. 이유를 나타내는 연결어들

우선 첫 번째로, + 절 / 두 번째로, + 절

- 왜 서울이 방문하기 좋은 곳인지에 대한 이유들이 많이 있습니다. 우선 첫 번째로, 세계적으로 좋은 박물관들과 문화명소들이 있습니다. 두 번째로, 음식들이 매우 환상적입니다.

첫 번째 이유는 + 절 / 두 번째 이유는 + 절

- 저는 제 아버지를 몇 가지 이유로 존경합니다. 첫 번째 이유는 아버지께서 헌신적이고 부지런한 분이시기 때문입니다. 두 번째 이유는 우리 가족을 사랑하고 뒷받침하기 위해 언제나 최선을 다하시기 때문입니다.

첫 번째는 + 명사구 / 두 번째는 + 명사구

- Big Money사의 마케팅 팀에 합류하는 데는 몇 가지 이점들이 있습니다. 첫 번째는 부서의 활기차고 협력적인 근무 분위기 입니다. 두 번째는 모든 직원에게 제공되는 감동적인 복리제도입니다.

2. Transitional Signals with Examples

For example, + CLAUSE

- I have many fond memories of my school days. For example, I will never forget the day my classmates threw a surprise party for me on my birthday.

For instance, + CLAUSE

- Whatever your interests, Seoul has something to offer you. For instance, if you enjoy musicals and plays, just head over to "University Road" for the latest performances.

… such as + NP…

- The market is filled with fresh fish and seafood such as squid, octopus and blowfish.

2. 예시를 나타내는 연결어

예를 들어, + 절

- 저는 학교에 대한 좋은 기억들을 많이 가지고 있습니다. 예를 들어, 저는 제 생일날 반 친구들이 열어 준 깜짝 파티를 절대로 잊지 못할 것입니다.

예를 들자면, + 절

- 당신의 관심사가 어떤 것이든, 서울은 당신에게 무언가를 제공할 수 있습니다. 예를 들어, 당신이 만약 뮤지컬과 연극을 좋아한다면, 최신 공연을 보기 위해 "대학로"를 향해 가면 됩니다.

… 와 같은 + 명사구…

- 시장에는 오징어, 문어 그리고 복어와 같은 신선한 생선과 해산물이 가득합니다.

Task 4

다음 세 개의 주제문장들을 읽고 연결어들을 사용해서 각각 두 번째 이유를 쓰시오.

1. Jeju Island is the best place to travel in Korea.
   The first reason is that the climate is always pleasant.
   ____

2. There are many good things about studying abroad.
   First of all, it is a great chance to improve your foreign language skills.
   ____
   ____

3. CUFS is superior to other online universities for several reasons.
   The first is the commitment of its faculty to quality education.
   ____

Task 5

빈칸에 예시를 보여주는 적절한 연결어들을 넣으시오. 필요하면 콤마를 쓰시오.

1. In Hong Kong, there is a great variety of different architectural styles. ___________ if you head to the far side of the island you can see old temples and other traditional buildings.

2. There are also many fine examples of modern architecture. ___________ in the main commercial district you can see several unique and inspiring skyscrapers.

3. Food is also a major drawing feature of the city. For those familiar with the type of Chinese food sold in Korea, popular foods ______________ dumplings and noodles can be found almost anywhere.

4. If you are feeling more adventurous however, head over to "Cao Cao's Revenge" for hot and spicy dishes _____ "Sichuan Hot Pot" and "Flower Pepper Lotus."

5. If you have children, there are a number of popular attractions available. ___________ Ocean Park is bound to keep your kids amused all day.

6. Finally, you can head back to the hotel after a long day of sightseeing to enjoy facilities _____ the indoor heated pool, the VIP massage room and our famous "Lucky Star" karaoke parlor.

WRAP-UP

1. Reasons and examples
   - A topic sentence and supporting sentences
   - Reasons and specific examples
2. Transitional signals with reasons
   - First of all, + CLAUSE / Second, + CLAUSE
   - The first reason is that + CLAUSE / The second reason is that + CLAUSE
   - The first is + NP / The second is + NP
3. Transitional signals with examples
   - For example, + CLAUSE
   - For instance, + CLAUSE
   - ...NP such as + NP...

1. 이유와 예시
   - 주제문과 뒷받침하는 문장들
2. 이유를 나타내는 연결어들
   - First of all, + 절 / Second, + 절
   - The first reason is that + 절 / The second reason is that + 절
   - The first is + 명사구 / The second is + 명사구
3. 예시를 나타내는 연결어들
   - For example, + 절
   - For instance, + 절
   - ...명사구 such as + 명사구...

Unit 11

Keeping in Touch with Family and Friends II

INTRODUCTION

Topic: Keeping in touch with family and friends
Writing Process: Editing a paragraph
Sentence Structure: Independent & dependent clauses, and subordinating conjunctions
Grammar: Kinds of sentences and fragments

주제: 가족, 친구들과 연락 주고 받기
쓰기: 단락 수정하기
구조: 독립 절과 종속절, 종속 접속사
문법: 문장의 종류, 불완전한 문장

WRITING PROCESS

1. Unedited paragraph

Dear Mr. Shin:

I am so excited that tomorrow is our 1st anniversary. I can't believe that we have been together for one year.
It feels like yesterday we first met. You haven't changed at all.

Except putting some weight.

I am still love you all my heart. I am sure that you are my Mr. Right.

We can't fly to aboard this time but do not be disappointed.

We can fly to Saipan next year.

Let's have a happy anniversary together.

With love Christina

2. Edited paragraph

Dear ~~Mr. Shin~~ Jaeseok,

Indent the first sentence.

I am so excited that tomorrow is our ~~1st~~ first anniversary. I can't believe that we have been together for ~~one~~ a whole year; ~~It~~ it feels like only yesterday when we first met. You haven't changed at all, ~~Except~~ except for putting on some weight. I ~~am~~ still love you with all my heart and I am sure that you are my Mr. Right. We can't fly ~~to~~ aboard this time but do not be disappointed. We can fly to Saipan next year. Let's have a happy anniversary together.

With love, Christina

3. Final paragraph

Dear Jaeseok,

I am so excited that tomorrow is our first anniversary. I can't believe that we have been together for a whole year; it feels like only yesterday when we first met. You haven't changed at all, except for putting on some weight.

I still love you with all my heart, and I am sure that you are my Mr. Right. We can't fly abroad this time but do not be disappointed. We can fly to Saipan next year. Let's have a happy anniversary together.

With love,
Christina

재석에게

나는 내일이 우리의 첫 번째 기념일이라는 것에 너무나 기분이 좋습니다. 나는 우리가 그 한 해를 쭉 함께 했다는 것을 믿을 수가 없습니다. 꼭 우리가 엊그제 만난 거 같은 기분이 들기 때문입니다. 당신은 살이 조금 찐 것을 제외하고는 변한 것이 없습니다.

나는 여전히 내 온 마음을 다해 당신을 사랑합니다. 그리고 나는 당신이 나의 천생연분이라는 것을 확신합니다. 우리는 이번엔 외국에 나갈 수는 없지만, 실망하지 않기로 해요. 우리는 내년에 사이판에 갈 수 있으니까요. 우리 같이 행복한 기념일을 보내기로 해요.

사랑을 담아,
크리스티나

Task 1 Editing awkward expressions

다음의 문단을 읽고, 밑줄 친 단어들을 알맞은 표현으로 바꾸시오.

(1) To. My sister

It is the first day of October. You must be at home with Hye-yun, my niece, (2) struggling daily routine. I wish I could give you a hand in taking care of her, but I cannot afford to do that because of my situation. I have been very busy with my work, and as you know, (3) my wife pregnant. For being a parent, I really respect you, and I am thankful to you for letting me know (4) that know how of being a good parent. But, what a surprise to hear about your second pregnancy. Congratulations, Sis! I am sure that our new babies will be good cousins to each other. I am always on your side, so just tell me whenever you need me.

Love,
Keeseok

(1) To. My sister → ______________________

(2) struggling daily routine → ______________________

(3) my wife pregnant → ______________________

(4) that know how of being → ______________________

SENTENCE STRUCTURE

Independent & Dependent clauses, and subordinating conjunctions

1. Independent & dependent clauses

A **clause** refers to a group of words that contains a subject and a verb. Not all clauses express a complete thought. There are two kinds of clauses. Clauses that express complete thoughts are called **independent clauses**. Clauses that do not express complete thoughts are called **dependent clauses**.

- Independent clause (IC) He is poor.
- Dependent clause (DC) ...because he is poor...

An independent clause has one SV combination and expresses a complete thought. It can stand by itself as a sentence. A simple sentence, for example, is an independent clause.

- Paris has excellent art exhibits.
- It was cloudy and windy yesterday.
- We finished the jigsaw puzzle and cleaned up the living room.

A dependent clause is an independent clause with a subordinating conjunction at the beginning of it.

- ...because it has excellent art exhibits...
- ...although it was cloudy and windy yesterday...
- ...after we finished the jigsaw puzzle and cleaned up the living room...

A dependent clause does not express a complete thought, so it cannot be a sentence by itself. It needs to be combined with an independent clause to make sense.

(IC) (DC)

- Art students should visit Paris because it has excellent art exhibits.
- We went on a picnic although it was windy and cold yesterday.
- We ate dinner after we finished the jigsaw puzzle and cleaned up the living room.

1. 독립절과 종속절

절은 주어와 동사를 담고 있는 단어들의 그룹을 말합니다. 모든 절이 완전한 생각을 나타내는 것은 아닙니다. 영어에는 두 가지 종류의 절이 있습니다. 완전한 생각을 표현하는 절을 독립절이라고 하고, 완전한 생각을 표현하지 않는 것을 종속절이라고 합니다.

- 독립절 그는 가난합니다.
- 종속절 그는 가난하기 때문에…

독립절은 하나의 주어-동사의 조합을 가지고 있으며, 완전한 생각을 표현합니다. 독립절은 그 자체가 문장이 될 수 있습니다. 단문은 독립절의 한 예입니다.

- 파리에서는 훌륭한 예술 전시회들이 열립니다.
- 어제는 날씨가 흐리고 바람이 불었습니다.
- 우리는 조각그림 맞추기를 끝내고 거실을 청소했습니다.

종속절은 독립절 앞에 종속접속사가 있는 절을 의미합니다.

- 그것이 훌륭한 예술 전시품들을 가지고 있었기 때문에…..
- 비록 어제 날씨가 흐리고 바람이 불었지만…..

• 우리가 조각그림 맞추기를 끝내고 거실 청소를 한 후에……

종속절은 완전한 생각을 표현하지 못하므로 단독으로는 온전한 문장을 구성할 수가 없습니다. 독립절과 함께 쓰여야 합니다.

• 파리엔 정말 훌륭한 예술 전시품들이 있기 때문에 예술을 전공하는 학생들은 파리를 방문해야만 합니다.
• 비록 어제 흐리고 바람이 불었지만, 우리는 소풍을 갔습니다.
• 우리는 조각그림 맞추기를 끝내고 거실을 청소한 후에, 저녁을 먹었습니다.

2. Subordinating conjunctions

There are various subordinating conjunctions (SC). Some introduce times, reasons, and others introduce contrasts and conditions.

• Reason: because, since, as
• Time: before, when, after, while, until
• Contrast: although, even though
• Condition: if, unless

Examples

• He cleaned the room **because** it was very messy.
• **When** I last heard from him, he was living in Dallas.
• They will be angry if I don't visit them.

Tips

1. Some subordinate conjunctions are also prepositions.
   • **after** the class is over (subordinating conjunction)

- **after** the class (preposition)
- **before** you eat breakfast (subordinating conjunction)
- **before** breakfast (preposition)

2. *Because* is a subordinate conjunction. *Because of* is a two-word preposition.
   - **because** I had a family emergency (subordinating conjunction)
   - **because of** a family emergency (preposition)

3. *While* is a subordinate conjunction. *During* is a preposition.
   - **While** I was watching the movie, I fell asleep. (subordinating conjunction)
   - What will you do **during** the summer vacation? (preposition)

2. 종속접속사

다양한 종속 접속사들이 있는데 어떤 것은 시간과 이유를 나타내고, 또 다른 것들은 대조와 조건을 나타냅니다.

종속접속사의 종류

- 이유: because, since, as (~하기 때문에)
- 시간: before (~전에), when(~때), after(~후에), while(~동안에), until(~할 때까지)
- 대조: although, even though (비록~이지만)
- 조건: if (만약~라면), unless (~하지 않는 한)

예시

방이 너무 더러워서 그는 그 방을 청소했습니다.
내가 마지막으로 그에게서 소식을 들었을 때, 그는 Dallas에 살고 있었습니다.
만약 그들을 방문하지 않는다면, 그들은 화를 낼 것입니다.

1. 몇몇 종속접속사들은 또한 전치사이기도 합니다.
   - 수업이 끝난 후에 (종속접속사)
   - 수업 후에 (전치사)
   - 당신이 아침을 먹기 전에 (종속접속사)
   - 아침을 먹기 전에 (전치사)

2. Because는 종속 접속사이지만 Because of 는 두 단어로 된 전치사입니다.
   - 내게 급한 집안 일이 생겨서 (종속 접속사)
   - 급한 집안 일 때문에 (전치사)

3. While은 접속사이고, during은 전치사입니다.
   - 나는 그 영화를 보는 동안에 잠이 들었습니다. (종속 접속사)
   - 여름 방학 동안에 당신은 무엇을 할 것입니까? (전치사)

Task 2

각각의 단어의 그룹이 독립 절(IC) 인지 종속절(DC) 인지 표시하시오.

	IC	DC
1. I take a walk around the block.	_____	_____
2. Before I go to work.	_____	_____
3. Yoga wakes up my body and clears my mind.	_____	_____
4. It's hard to do this in the winter.	_____	_____
5. Because it is still dark when I go to work.	_____	_____

Task 3

각각의 문장에서 종속접속사를 찾아 쓰시오.

1. Wait for a green light before you cross the street. ________
2. I will go straight to bed after I finish this workout. ________
3. My neighbors were having a party while I was trying to sleep. ________
4. Although he lived in Florida for many years, my father doesn't speak English ________
5. I will be happy if my boyfriend buys me flowers for Valentine's Day. ________

Task 4

각각의 종속절을 가지고 문장을 완성하시오.

1. Before I go to school
   → ______________________________ before I go to school.

2. Because it is late when I get home
   → ____________________ because it is late when I get home.

3. Although I try to get up early even on weekends
   → Although I try to get up early even on weekends, __________.

4. I become moody and depressed

→ ____

5. If I skip a meal

→ ____

GRAMMAR

Kinds of sentences and fragments

Kinds of sentences

Simple sentence (one independent clause)

- I felt exhausted.
- I went to bed.
- I stayed up.

Compound sentence

(two or more independent clauses joined with a comma and a coordinating conjunction)

- I felt exhausted, so I went to bed.
- I felt exhausted, but I stayed up to finish my homework.
- I felt exhausted, and I really wanted to go to bed, but I stayed up to finish my homework.

Complex Sentence

(one independent clause plus one or more dependent clauses)

- I went to bed because I was exhausted.
- Since I was exhausted, I went to bed.
- Although I was exhausted, I stayed up to finish my homework.

문장의 종류

<u>단문</u> (하나의 독립된 문장)

- 나는 완전히 지쳤습니다.
- 나는 자러 갔습니다.
- 나는 깨어있었습니다.

<u>중문</u> (쉼표와 접속사로 연결된 두 개 또는 그 이상의 독립절)

- 나는 지쳤습니다. 그래서 자러 갔습니다.
- 나는 지쳤습니다. 그러나 나의 숙제를 끝내기 위해 깨어있었습니다.
- 나는 지쳤습니다 그리고 나는 정말 자러 가고 싶었습니다. 그렇지만 나의 숙제를 끝내기 위해 깨어 있었습니다.

<u>복문</u> (하나의 독립절과 하나 또는 그 이상의 종속절로 이루어진 문장)

- 나는 지쳤기 때문에 자러 갔습니다.
- 내가 지쳤기 때문에 자러 갔습니다.
- 비록 나는 지쳤지만, 내 숙제를 끝내기 위해 깨어있었습니다.

2. Fragments – dependent clauses

A sentence fragment is a part of a sentence. Dependent clauses are fragments, and they are not sentences. A dependent clause must be combined with an independent clause to be a sentence.

Examples

- Because he is thirsty for success.
- When the movie ended.
- Although she exercises constantly.

Repair Jobs:

- Because he is thirsty for success, he spends all his free time studying.
- When the movie ended, we went to get ice cream.
- Although she exercises constantly, she never loses any weight.

문장의 일부 – 종속절

Fragment는 문장의 일부를 의미합니다. 종속절도 문장의 일부이지, 완전한 문장이 아닙니다. 종속절은 독립 절과 결합해야만 문장이 될 수 있습니다.

예시

- 그가 성공에 목말라 있었기 때문에
- 영화가 끝났을 때
- 비록 그녀가 계속해서 운동을 하지만

수정 작업:

- 그가 성공에 목말라 있었기 때문에, 그는 그의 모든 여가 시간을 공부하는데 씁니다.
- 영화가 끝났을 때, 우리는 아이스크림을 사러 갔습니다.
- 비록 그녀가 계속해서 운동을 하지만, 그녀는 체중이 전혀 줄지 않습니다.

Task 5

다음의 문장들이, 단문(simple), 중문(compound) 또는 복문(complex)인지를 구분하고, 각각의 독립 절에 밑줄을 그으시오.

1. Many people like to stay at home when they have time off.
   → _____, Many people like to stay at home when they have time off.

2. Some people like to visit relatives, and others like to travel abroad.
   → _____, Some people like to visit relatives, and others like to travel abroad.

3. Lately "extreme" vacations are becoming more and more popular.
   → _____, Lately "extreme" vacations are becoming more and more popular.

4. For instance, some extreme vacationers go alligator hunting in Australia or bungee jumping in New Zealand.
   → _____, For instance, some extreme vacationers go alligator hunting in Australia or bungee jumping in New Zealand.

5. Some people enjoy spending their holiday indoors with a good book, while others spend their free time doing volunteer work.
   → _____, Some people enjoy spending their holiday indoors with a good book, while others spend their free time doing volunteer work.

6. Opportunities for volunteer work are increasing because so many people in the world need help.
   → _____, Opportunities for volunteer work are increasing because so many people in the world need help.

7. Students often want to make the most of their time, so they spend their vacations cramming for examinations.
   → _____, Students often want to make the most of their time, so they spend their vacations cramming for examinations.

Task 6

각각의 항목에 문장의 일부(F)인지, 또는 완전한 문장(S)인지를 쓰고, 문장의 일부는 완전한 문장으로 쓰시오.

1. Because so many students missed the exam
   → ______________________________

2. Before I eat breakfast
   → ______________________________

3. Because I forgot my umbrella, I got sick.
   → ______________________________

4. Because she was out all night dancing
   → ______________________________

5. Since she works so hard and never misses a class.

→ ______________________________

6. Whenever he gets sick.

→ ______________________________

7. He seems to come late only when there is a test.

→ ______________________________

WRAP-UP

1. Independent and dependent clauses
   - Independent clauses express a complete thought.
   - Dependent clauses do not express a complete thought.

2. Subordinating conjunctions
   - because, since, as
   - before, when, after, while, until
   - although, even though
   - if, unless

3. Kinds of sentences
   - Simple sentence
   - Compound sentence
   - Complex sentence

4. Fragments-dependent clause

1. 독립절과 종속절
   - 독립절은 완전한 생각을 표현한다.
   - 종속절은 완전한 생각을 표현하지 않는다.

2. 종속접속사
   - 이유: because, since, as (~하기 때문에)
   - 시간: before (~전에), when(~때), after(~후에), while(~동안에), until(~할 때까지)
   - 대조: although, even though (비록~이지만)
   - 조건: if (만약~라면), unless (만약 ~하지 않으면)

3. 문장 종류
   - 단문
   - 중문
   - 복문

4. 문장의 일부 – 종속절

Unit 12

Expressing Opinions

INTRODUCTION

Topic: Expressing opinions
Writing Process: Facts & opinions, and transition signals for opinions
Grammar: Adjective clauses with *who*, *which*, and *that*

주제: 의견 표현하기
쓰기: 사실 & 의견, 의견을 나타내는 연결어
문법: who, which, that과 함께 오는 형용사절

OUR LIFE

Setting: Teachers lounge, Super Duper English
Characters: Katherine, Fred

Kathy : Hey Fred, how was class?
Fred : Oh, it was okay. Actually the kids seemed really exhausted today.
Kathy : Yeah, it was the same in my class. I think they have exams this week or something.

Fred : Huh? Nobody mentioned anything about exams to *me.* What kind of test are we supposed to give?

Kathy : Us? No, *we* don't give exams. They are taking tests at school. You know, their regular school.

Fred : Ah···got it. Wait a second···so these kids are going to public school every day, then after school they come here and keep on studying?

Kathy : Duh! You didn't know that?

Fred : I guess I just never thought about it before. I haven't been here for that long, you know.

Kathy : Well, that's how they do things here. You have to hit the books nonstop from morning till night.

Fred : Wow, I'm impressed! When I have kids I should just raise them here in Korea.

Kathy : Bring them up in Korea? Are you crazy? Do you want your children to be deprived of a childhood?

Fred : What do you mean?

Kathy : I mean these kids never get a chance to be kids. They're so busy studying they don't have time to run around, play with their friends, have fun···you know, the stuff kids do.

Fred : Come on, isn't that going a little too far? After all, our students here are really smart – way more advanced than the students back home. Something must be working, right?

Kathy : You have a point, but think about those students back in the States – they play sports, they do art, they participate in after-school clubs and activities. Students are more well-rounded there.

Fred : I don't know what students *you're* talking about – the students *I* taught in New York did nothing but watch TV, play video games and eat junk food all day long. Don't you think it's better to keep them in the classroom?

Kathy : Well…perhaps in some cases, yes. But on the other hand, good education doesn't come cheap, you know. Parents in Korea spend exorbitant sums on their children's education. It's like education just sucks all their money away.

Fred : I see what you mean. Then again, the money you put toward your children's education could be considered an investment, too, right?

Fade away with mutual laughter and corny sitcom music.

Translation

배경 : Super Duper 영어학원 교사라운지

인물 : Katherine, Fred

Kathy: Fred! 수업은 어땠어?

Fred : 괜찮았어. 그런데 오늘 학생들이 정말 피곤해 보이긴 하더라.

Kathy: 응, 내 수업 시간에도 그랬어. 내 생각엔 이번 주에 시험이 있는 것 같아.

Fred : 그래? 나한테는 아무도 시험에 대해서 얘기하지 않았는데. 우리가 어떤 시험을 만들어야 하는데?

Kathy: 우리? 아니 우리가 시험을 만드는 것이 아니라 아이들이 정규학교에서 시험을 본다는 말이야.

Fred : 아, 알겠다. 잠시만, 그렇다면 아이들은 매일 정규학교를 가고 그 후에 여기에 와서 계속 공부를 한다는 말이야?

Kathy: 너 설마 몰랐어?

Fred : 아마도 한번도 이거에 대해서 깊게 생각해 본적이 없는 것 같아. 너도 알다시피 내가 여기서 그렇게 오래 일한 것도 아니고 말이야.

Kathy: 음, 여기서는 보통 그렇게 공부해. 아침부터 저녁까지 멈추지 않고 책과 씨름 해야 하지.

Fred : 와, 대단하데! 나중에 아이를 가지면 한국에서 길러야겠어.

Kathy: 한국에서 아이를 기를 거라고? 제정신이야? 네 아이가 불우한 어린 시절을 보내길 원하는 거야?

Fred : 무슨 뜻이야?

Kathy: 아이들이 아이다워 질 기회조차 없잖아. 공부하느라 너무 바빠서 뛰어 놀거나 친구들과 어울리는 거와 같은 아이들이 하는 그런 것들을 할 시간이 없잖아.

Fred : 에이, 그 정도까지는 아니지 않아? 결국에는 여기 있는 학생들이 미국에 있는 학생들 보다 훨씬 더 똑똑하고 고등수준인걸 보면 한국에서의 교육이 뭔가 좋다는 것이 아닐까?

Kathy: 무슨 말하는지는 알겠는데 미국에 있는 학생들을 생각해 봐봐. 그 아이들은 운동도 하고 미술도 하고 방과후에 있는 동아리 활동에 참여도 하잖아. 그 아이들이 더 다재 다능하다고.

Fred : 네가 말하는 학생들을 난 모르겠어. 내가 뉴욕에서 가르쳤던 학생들은 TV 보고, 비디오 게임하고, 하루 종일 인스턴트 음식만 먹는 아이들이었다고. 차라리 교실에서 공부만 하는 아이들이 더 낫다고 생각하지 않아?

Kathy: 음....아마도 어떤 경우에는 그렇다고 생각해. 또 다른 면에서 보면 좋은 교육은 비용이 들지. 한국에 있는 부모들은 엄청난 수입을 자녀교육비용에 쏟아 붓잖아. 돈을 전부 빨아들이는 교육이라고.

Fred : 무슨 말인지 알겠어. 하지만 자녀 교육비로 쏟아 붓는 돈은 일종의 투자와도 같은 거야 그렇지 않아?

서로의 웃음소리와 시트콤 음악과 함께 장면이 사라진다.

Words & expressions

① okay (=soso)	그냥 그래
② exhausted	피곤한
③ huh? (colloquial)	엉?
④ mention something about	~에 대해서 언급하다
⑤ get it (=understand)	이해하다

⑥ public school vs. private school (UK: <u>state</u> school vs. <u>public</u> shool)	공립학교 vs 사립학교 (영국에선 공립학교를 State school 사립학교를 public school이라고 한다)
⑦ keep V-ing vs. keep on V-ing	계속 ~하다
⑧ duh (colloquial)	설마
⑨ I never thought about it before (colloquial) vs. I <u>have</u> never thought about it before	지금까지 한 번도 생각해 본적이 없다
⑩ hit the books	책과 씨름하다
⑪ nonstop	멈추지 않고
⑫ from morning till night	아침부터 저녁까지
⑬ I'm impressed (vs. that's impressive)	감명받다 (vs 감동적인)
⑭ raise / bring up	기르다 / 양육하다
⑮ deprive A of B / A be deprived of B	A에게 서 B를 빼앗기다 / A가 B를 빼앗기다
⑯ go too far	(상식 등에서) 지나치다
⑰ way more (colloquial, means 'far more')	훨씬 더
⑱ be working (=be having a positive effect)	좋은 결과가 있는
⑲ You have a point (debate rhetoric)	당신 말도 맞는 것 같아요
⑳ after-school clubs / after-school activities (also cf. extracurricular activities)	방과후 동아리 활동 / 방과후 활동 (과외활동)
㉑ well-rounded	다재 다능한
㉒ do nothing but ~	~하기만 하다
㉓ perhaps in some cases, yes (debate rhetoric)	어떤 경우에는 맞다 (토론 등에서)
㉔ on the other hand (debate rhetoric)	반면에
㉕ ~ doesn't come cheap (colloquial)	싸게 되지 않다
㉖ exorbitant sums	엄청난 수입
㉗ put money toward ~	돈을 어디에 넣다
㉘ be considered ~ (<u>not</u> 'be considered as ~')	~로 간주되다

Comprehension questions

1. According to Fred, how did his class go on this day?
   (1) It was excellent.
   (2) It was good.
   (3) It was so-so.
   (4) It was terrible.

2. Which word best describes Fred's students on this day?
   (1) psyched
   (2) tired
   (3) depressed
   (4) hopeful

3. Why does Fred want to raise his children in Korea?
   (1) He loves Korean food.
   (2) He thinks Korean teachers are better.
   (3) He believes Korea has the best schools.
   (4) He is impressed with Korean study habits.

4. Which word best describes Katherine's attitude toward Korean education?
   (1) impressed
   (2) skeptical
   (3) optimistic
   (4) frightened

5. What is Katherine's impression of American students?
   (1) They work too hard.
   (2) They are always playing sports.
   (3) Their interests are diverse.
   (4) They are very intelligent.

WRITING PROCESS

Facts & opinions, and transition signals for opinions

1. Facts & opinions

Now we will learn to express an opinion and then support it with facts. Opinions are statements of one's beliefs. Opinions begin with, "I believe..." or "I think that..." They are different from facts because people can disagree with opinions. They may or may not be true. Facts are statements that everybody should agree with.

Fact	Opinion
• She has two sons and one daughter.	• Her daughter is really beautiful.
• Mr. Kim said, "I am a good father."	• Mr. Kim is a good father.

Although the second sentence on the left may seem like an opinion, it is a fact, because it is a fact that Mr. Kim said something.

When you write an opinion paragraph, your topic sentence is your opinion. Using facts to support your ideas will strengthen your paragraph.

2. Transition signals for opinions

When stating an opinion, you should indicate that it is an opinion by using a transition expression.

- In my opinion,
- In my view,

- From my point of view,
- I believe
- It is my belief (that)
- I think (that)
- There is no doubt (that)
- In my opinion, everyone should go to college.
- I believe that a Kia is better than a Daewoo.

The first transition signal is followed by a comma. The second does not have a comma, and you may delete the connecting word, *that.*

To give information from an outside source (a newspaper, book, another person), use *according to* with a comma.

According to (sth/sb),

- According to Megan, Pizza Hut has the best cheese pizza.
- According to the advertisement, what is cost of the Business Cruise package?

1. 사실과 의견

이제 의견을 표현하는 방법과 그것을 사실로 지지하는 방법을 배우겠습니다. 의견은 개인의 믿음의 진술입니다. 의견은 "나는 ~라고 믿는다" 또는 "내 생각에는" 로 시작합니다. 의견은 다른 사람들이 동의하지 않을 수 있다는 점에서 사실과 다릅니다. 의견은 사실일수도, 사실이 아닐 수도 있습니다. 사실은 모두가 동의해야만 하는 진술입니다.

사실	의견
• 그녀는 아들 두 명과 딸 한 명이 있다.	• 그녀의 딸은 정말 아름답다.
• 김씨가 말했다,"나는 좋은 아빠야."	• 김씨는 좋은 아빠이다.

왼쪽 두 번째 문장은 의견처럼 보이지만 김씨가 말한 것이기 때문에 사실이라고 볼 수 있습니다. 의견에 대해서 쓸 때, 주제 문장은 당신의 의견입니다. 그 의견을 뒷받침 해주기 위해서 사실을 쓴다면 문단은 더욱 탄탄해질 것이다.

2. 의견을 나타내는 연결어

의견에 대해서 진술할 때 연결어를 사용함으로 이것이 의견임을 나타내는 것이 좋습니다.

- 내 의견으로는,
- 내 관점에서 보면,
- 내 견해로는.
- 나는 ~라고 믿습니다
- ~라는 것이 내 믿음입니다
- 나는~라고 생각합니다
- ~에 대해서 의심할 여지가 없습니다
- 내 의견으로는 모두가 대학에 가야 합니다.
- 나는 기아가 대우보다 낫다고 믿습니다.

첫 번째 연결어 다음에는 쉼표가 옵니다. 두 번째 연결어 다음에는 쉼표가 오지 않으며 접속사 *that*은 생략 가능합니다.

정보의 출처가 신문, 책, 다른 사람인 경우에는 쉼표와 함께 "~에 의하면" 을 씁니다.

~에 의하면,

- Megan에 의하면, 피자헛이 가장 맛있는 치즈피자를 만듭니다.
- 광고에 따르면, 비지니스 크루즈 패키지의 가격이 얼마입니까?

Task 1

다음의 단락을 읽고 질문에 답하시오.

I do not think that capital punishment is right. Firstly, I think all killing is wrong. Human beings do not have the right to deprive each other of life. Only God can do that, not the government. Since the government is made up of people, it should not kill somebody, even if that person has committed a horrible crime. Secondly, the threat of execution does not prevent crime. No criminals plan on getting caught at all, so they will do what they want to do regardless of the possible consequences. In fact, the murder rate of a city can even rise during times of increased state executions, which is exactly what happened in New Orleans in 1987. Third, and most importantly, with advances in science and technology it is not uncommon for new evidence to appear which vindicates somebody who has already been convicted of a crime. If this happens with somebody who has been executed however, there is simply no way to turn back the clock. Although this might seem more like a Hollywood plotline than reality, in the U.S. alone more than twenty people were executed by mistake in the twentieth century, and that is only the number of verified cases. In my opinion, these cases can be considered acts of murder by the government. In a word, capital punishment should be banned.

1. What does the writer say about capital punishment?
   a. that it's wrong
   b. that it's right
   c. that it's neither right nor wrong
   d. none of the above

2. Is the writer's view on capital punishment a fact or opinion?
   a. fact
   b. opinion

3. How many reasons does the writer give?
   a. 1
   b. 2
   c. 3
   d. 4

4. Of the reasons that the writer gives, how many are facts?
   a. 0
   b. 1
   c. 2
   d. 3

5. Are all the details that the writer gives facts or opinions?
   a. they are all facts
   b. no, some are opinions

Task 2

여러분의 의견을 이용해 연결어(transition signal) 뒷부분을 완성 하세요.

1. In my view, ______________________________.
2. I believe that______________________________.
3. I think that ______________________________.
4. In my opinion, ___________________________.
5. According to__________,____________________.

Task 3

아래 주제에 대한 의견을 쓰시오. 모든 문장에 연결어(transition signal)를 쓰시오.

Topic: The minimum age for drinking in Korea.

Opinion: ____

Support: _________________________________ (fact/opinion)

Support: _________________________________ (fact/opinion)

GRAMMAR

Adjective clauses with *who, which*, and *that*

An adjective clause is a dependent clause that modifies a noun. An adjective clause generally follows the word or words it modifies. An adjective clause is usually introduced by a relative pronoun such as *who*, *which* or *that*.

Who refers only to people, *which* refers only to things, and *that* refers to people or things.

Examples:

- Steve Jobs was a person who had immense creativity.
- Steve Jobs was a person that had a boundless imagination.
- The people who know the least always say the most.
- The people that have the least knowledge always speak the loudest.
- In the new system, even a team which has never won a game still has a chance to enter the final round.
- Under the new rules, the team that is in last place still has a chance to win.

Commas are used with nonrestrictive clauses. A nonrestrictive clause contains information that can be omitted without affecting the sentence's basic meaning.

Who and *which* can be used in a nonrestrictive clause.

Examples:

- I will never forget my first teacher, who was one of the kindest people I have ever met.

- Emily, <u>who</u> can play many instruments, taught me how to play the flute.
- Young children shouldn't watch Jurassic Park, <u>which</u> has a lot of violence.
- The contract was cancelled, <u>which</u> was what he wanted.

who, which, that 이 이끄는 형용사절 (관계대명사절)

형용사절은 명사를 꾸며주는 종속절입니다.
일반적으로, 형용사절은 그것이 꾸미는 단어나 단어들 다음에 오게 됩니다.
형용사절은 대개 *who, which, that*과 같은 관계대명사가 이끌게 됩니다.

*Who*는 사람만을 지칭하고, *which*는 사물만을 지칭합니다. 그리고 *that*은 사람이나 사물을 지칭합니다.

예:

- Steve Jobs는 엄청난 독창력을 가졌던 사람이었습니다.
- Steve Jobs는 무한한 상상력을 가졌던 사람이었습니다.
- 가장 적게 아는 사람이 항상 가장 많이 이야기합니다.
- 가장 적은 지식을 가지고 있는 사람이 항상 가장 크게 이야기합니다
- 새로운 제도에서는, 한번도 이겨보지 못한 팀 조차도 마지막 라운드에 들어갈 수 있는 기회를 가지게 됩니다. .
- 새로운 규칙아래에, 꼴찌인 팀도 여전히 이길 기회를 가지고 있다.

콤마들은 비제한적 관계사절과 함께 쓰이게 됩니다. 비제한적 관계사절은 문장의 기본적인 의미를 손상시키지 않으면서 생략 가능한 정보들을 포함한다. Who와 which가 비제한적 관계사절에서 쓰입니다.

예:

- 나는 첫 번째 선생님을 잊지 못하는데, 그분은 지금까지 내가 만나본 가장

친절한 사람들 중에 한 명이었습니다.

- Emily는 많은 악기들을 연주할 수 있는데, 나에게 오보에 부는 법을 가르쳐 주었습니다.
- 어린아이들은 Jurassic Park을 보아서는 안됩니다. 그 영화에는 폭력적인 장면이 많이 나옵니다.
- 그 계약은 취소되었는데, 그것은 그가 원하던 것이었습니다.

Task 4

Who 나 which을 써서 빈칸을 채우시오.

1. In traditional marriages, _____ are still quite common in many countries, your future spouse is chosen by somebody else.

2. Sometimes the mother and father, _____ know their children better than they know themselves, make the choice.

3. In other places, the decision is made by a matchmaker, _____ is paid to look for an appropriate partner.

4. It is common for the new couple to feel awkward at their first meeting, _____ often occurs in the presence of the parents.

5. Arranged marriages don't necessarily mean a lack of freedom. A man or woman _____ is unsatisfied with the chosen partner can usually request another.

6. Romantic marriages, _____ are common in the western world, often turn out unsuccessfully.

7. People _____ marry "for love" are more likely to get divorced than people in arranged marriages, _____ seem to be more stable.

Task 5

Who나 which으로 시작하는 형용사절을 써서 각 문장을 완성하시오.

1. My hometown, ____, is a wonderful place.

2. I will always be grateful to my mother, ______________________.

3. Dr. Sung Eungyeong, ______________________________, is the professor of this course.

4. Mt. Halla, ____________________________________, is located on Jeju Island.

5. The ninth president of Korea was No Muhyeon, ______________.

6. The IAFF 2011 World Championships were held in Daegu, ________________________.

WRAP-UP

1. Facts and opinions
2. Transition signals for opinions
    - In my opinion,
    - In my view,
    - From my point of view,
    - I believe
    - It is my belief (that)
    - I think (that)
    - There is no doubt (that)
    - According to (sth/sb),
3. Adjective clauses with *who, which*, and *that*
    - dependent clauses modifying a noun.
    - following the modified word or words
    - being introduced by a relative pronoun such as *who*, *which* or *that*.

1. 사실과 의견
2. 의견을 나타내는 연결어
    - 내 의견으로는,
    - 내 관점으로는,
    - 내 견해로는,
    - 나는 ~라고 믿는다.
    - 나는 ~라고 생각한다.
    - ~에는 의심할 여지가 없다.
    - ~에 따르면,
3. *who, which*, 그리고 *that*과 함께 쓰이는 형용사절(관계사절)
    - 명사를 수식하는 종속절
    - 수식하는 단어 뒤에 옴
    - *who*, *which* or *that* 과 같은 관계대명사로 시작함

Unit 13

Review

Unit 8

Exploring Social Issues I

1. Listing-order paragraphs
2. Listing-order transition signals
   - First,... / Second,... / Third,... / Fourth,...
   - ...also... / Also...
   - First of all,...
   - In addition,...
   - Furthermore,...
3. Adverbs
   - Adverbs modifying verbs
   - Adverbs modifying adjectives
   - Adverbs modifying other adverbs

1. 나열순서에 따라 단락 쓰기
2. 나열순서 전환 신호들
   - First,... / Second,... / Third,... / Fourth,...
   - ...also... / Also,...

- First of all,...
- In addition,...
- Furthermore,...

3. 부사
   - 동사들을 수식하는 부사들
   - 형용사들을 수식하는 부사들
   - 다른 부사들을 수식하는 부사들

Task 1

아래의 상자에서 적절한 단어나 표현을 골라 각 문장을 완성하시오.

depressed	confusing	insist that
make sense	appropriate	catch on
What's wrong?	manners	somehow
some kind of		

(1) Even though you are not feeling well, I _____ you go to school today.

(2) Our professor said that the correct answer is C, but that answer doesn't _____.

(3) It took me a while to understand the system here, but I finally managed to _____.

(4) Number eleven was the most _____ question on the exam.

(5) She takes a nap whenever she feels _____.

Task 2

아래 단락에 나열순서를 나타내는 연결어들을 모두 찾아 쓰시오.

Cats make the best pets for three reasons. First of all, cats are very independent. Aside from feeding and cleaning the litter box, you can rest easy that a cat will take care of itself. Second, they are clean. If a cat isn't sleeping or playing, it is most likely licking its fur or cleaning itself. Also, cats don't need baths since they clean themselves. Third, cats are very quiet. They don't bark but purr, which is very quiet. In addition, they can help you relax, which isn't a bad thing.

1. ________________
2. ________________
3. ________________
4. ________________
5. ________________

Task 3

여러분이 좋아하는 취미들을 떠올려 보시오. 적어도 3개의 취미들을 나열한 단락을 쓰시오. 그 취미들이 좋은 까닭도 쓰시오. 단락쓰기를 할 때, 나열순서 연결어들을 사용하시오.

Task 4

아래 상자에 있는 단어를 사용해 각 문장을 적절하게 완성하시오.

good	well	passionate	passionately
hard	terrible	terribly	wonderful
wonderfully	hardly		

(1) That new comedy got great reviews, but I found it _____ boring.

(2) You have to work _____ if you want to succeed.

(3) I am impressed by how _____ she is about everything she does.

(4) His new painting came out _____. The colors and textures are amazing.

(5) I'm really _____ at English, but I can't do math very _____.

Unit 9

Exploring Social Issues II

1. Editing a paragraph: An Ideal Husband
2. Topic sentence
    - Topic + controlling idea
3. Supporting sentences
    - Support the idea of the topic sentence
    - Be relevant to the main idea
4. Concluding sentence
    - Close the paragraph

- Restate the topic

5. Run on sentences
    - Incorrect punctuation or absence of conjunctions
6. Repairing run-on sentences
    - Put a period (or semicolon) between the two sentences, making two separate sentences.
    - Add a comma and coordinating conjunction, making a compound sentence.

1. 단락 수정하기: 이상적인 남편
2. 주제 문장
    - 주제 + 통제하는 아이디어
3. 뒷받침하는 문장들
    - 주제 문장의 생각 뒷받침 하기
    - 주제와 연관성이 있어야 함
4. 결론 문장
    - 단락 마무리하기
    - 주제 재언급하기
5. 계속되는 문장들
    - 잘못된 구두점 또는 접속사의 부재
6. 계속되는 문장들 수정하기
    - 두 문장들 사이에 점(또는 세미콜론) 넣어서 두 문장을 독립된 문장들로 만들기
    - 콤마와 접속사를 더해 중문으로 만들기

Task 5

질문을 읽고 알맞은 답을 고르세요.

1. Which of the following is a topic sentence?
   (1) In summer, you can go to the beach.
   (2) Korea has many outdoor activities available to everyone.
   (3) In the winter, you can go skiing.
   (4) In the fall, you can go on a hike to view autumn foliage.

2. Look at this sentence:
   Good teachers always listen to their students.
   What is the topic?
   (1) Good teachers
   (2) Students

3. Look at this sentence:
   Artistic talent and mathematical ability are two qualities of a good architect.
   What is the controlling idea?
   (1) a good architect
   (2) artistic talent and mathematical ability

4. A topic sentence tells the reader what they are going to read.
   a. TRUE
   b. FALSE

5. A controlling idea tells the reader what will be discussed about the topic in the paragraph.
   a. TRUE
   b. FALSE

Task 6

각각의 단락에서 관계없는 문장을 찾아서 아래에 쓰시오.

1. My parents gave me a Canon AE-1 camera when I graduated from high school a hundred years ago. I'm thinking about taking it to a camera shop and having it cleaned and checked-out. It also matches my laptop. It's in great shape, but I haven't touched it since roughly 1995. Can a person still buy film at a regular store? Is it still in production? For some reason I like the idea of using that great old camera again.

   → ______________________________

2. Over the weekend I want to work on my Twitter and Facebook pages. It's cool to hang out with friends. My Facebook page has especially been neglected, and I want to do a little weed-whacking and raking, and get things back in order over there. Twitter, too. I like both, but go through periods when I don't. I want to be more consistent.

   → ______________________________

3. My favorite Korean film is 'Welcome to Dongmakgol.' If I had a foreign friend, I would recommend this film. This film has the history of Korea, the sadness of the division, and love and friendship beyond ideology. The setting of this film is when it's near the end of the Korean War. Some South Korean soldiers and some North Korean soldiers met at Dongmakgol in war. Dongmakgol is the untouched land that is like a virgin forest. South Korea and North Korean have different ideologies, but they shared one in this film. That was to save that village. The village also grows lots of vegetables.

   → ______________________________

Task 7

다음 계속되는 문장들을 올바르게 고쳐서 다시 쓰시오.

(1) She licked the stamp and stuck it on the envelope and dropped the letter in the box.

→ ______________________________

(2) The new manager is quite young he has more experience than the old manager.

→ ______________________________

(3) My new phone has a beautiful display it has great apps I love it.

→ ______________________________

(4) I will finish this job after it's done I will call you.

→ ______________________________

Task 8

다음의 문장들을 수정한 후, 하나의 단락으로 만드세요.

(1) Cats and dogs both make great pets they provide joy to many families.
(2) However they don't get along well if you want a pet you must choose one or the other.
(3) The animal might live with your family for several years it is important to make your choice wisely.

(4) Some people enjoy winning the affection of a cat others prefer the steady loyalty of a dog.

(5) You can get advice about pets from friends and classmates if you need it ultimately the choice is yours to make.

Unit 10

Keeping in Touch with Family and Friends I

1. Reasons and examples
2. Transitional signals with reasons
   - First of all, + CLAUSE / Second, + CLAUSE
   - The first reason is that + CLAUSE / The second reason is that + CLAUSE
   - The first is + NP / The second is + NP
3. Transitional signals with examples
   - For example, + CLAUSE
   - For instance, + CLAUSE
   - ...NP such as + NP...

1. 이유와 예시
2. 이유를 나타내는 연결어들
   - First of all, + 절 / Second, + 절
   - The first reason is that + 절 / The second reason is that + 절
   - The first is + 명사구 / The second is + 명사구
3. 예시를 나타내는 연결어들
   - For example, + 절
   - For instance, + 절
   - …명사구 such as + 명사구…

Task 9

아래의 상자에서 적절한 단어나 표현을 찾아 각 문장을 완성시키시오.

psyched	as soon as	intense
keep in touch	or something	inevitable
pretty much	speaking of	all the time
not an option		

(1) Hurry up! We can leave _____ you finish your homework.

(2) I try to _____ with all my friends, but it's hard to find the time.

(3) Everyone is so _____ about the trip – I really hope it isn't cancelled.

(4) Failure is _____ this time. If you don't do the job right, you will be fired!

(5) _____ birthdays, isn't yours coming up next month?

Task 10

예시 단락을 읽고 개요를 완성하시오.

The Advantages of Living in Korea

Nowadays, living in Korea has become an enjoyable experience. First, the capital Seoul has become a cosmopolitan city. Seoul offers all the comforts of modern life, including technology. Also, the culture in Seoul is very diverse and there are many arts and events that reflect this diversity. Second, it is easy to travel, wherever you are in Korea. In every city there are buses and subways that connect you to just about every corner of the map. You can also enjoy a trip on the KTX that will take you to any of the major cities in Korea. Korea is truly a wonderful place to live.

__________________________(Title)

Topic Sentence: ____

Reason A: ____

Example 1:______________________________________

Example 2:______________________________________

Reason B: ____

Example 1:______________________________________

Example 2:______________________________________

Concluding Sentence:____________________________________

Task 11

다음 주제를 읽고 개요를 완성하시오.

Why cities are better than the countryside (Title)
Topic Sentence: Cities are better to live in than the countryside

Reason A: ______________________________

Example 1: ______________________________

Example 2: ______________________________

Reason B: ______________________________

Example 1: ______________________________

Example 2: ______________________________

Concluding Sentence: ______________________________

Task 12

아래의 상자에서 적절한 단어나 표현을 찾아 각 문장을 완성 하시오.

first of all	second	the first is
the second	for example	such as

(1) We offer a broad range of exciting courses __________ "World English" and "Dynamic Assessment."

(2) There are many reasons why Korean dramas are so popular. __________ that the plots are so exciting and addictive. __________, the stars are so attractive and charming.

(3) Many delicious, exotic fruits can be found in Puerto Rico. __________, mangos grow wild on trees all around the island.

(4) There are two basic reasons why our new vacuum cleaner is the best product on the market. _____, it is so small and compact. __________ reason is that it sucks harder than any other available model.

Unit 11

Keeping in Touch with Family and Friends II

1. Independent and dependent clauses
   - Independent clauses express a complete thought.
   - Dependent clauses do not express a complete thought.
2. Subordinating conjunctions
   - because, since, as
   - before, when, after, while, until
   - although, even though
   - if, unless
3. Kinds of sentences
   - Simple sentence
   - Compound sentence
   - Complex Sentence
4. Fragments-dependent clause

1. 독립절과 종속절
   - 독립절은 완전한 생각을 표현한다.
   - 종속절은 완전한 생각을 표현하지 않는다.
2. 종속접속사
   - 이유: because, since, as (~하기 때문에)
   - 시간: before (~전에), when(~때), after(~후에), while(~동안에), until(~할 때까지)
   - 대조: although, even though (비록~이지만)
   - 조건: if (만약~라면), unless (만약 ~하지 않으면)
3. 문장 종류
   - 단문
   - 중문
   - 복문
4. 불완전한 문장 – 종속절

Task 13

다음 각 절이 독립절 (IC) 인지 혹은 종속절 (DC) 인지 표시하시오.

	IC	DC
1. I take a stroll around the park.	_____	_____
2. Before I go home.	_____	_____
3. Jogging wakes up my body and clears my mind.	_____	_____
4. It's hard to do this in the summer.	_____	_____
5. Because it is still fun.	_____	_____

Task 14

다음 각 문장에서 종속 접속사를 찾아 쓰시오.

1. Wait for the person to finish talking before you add your two cents. __________
2. I will go home after I finish this meeting. __________
3. My friend was calling me while I was in the shower. __________
4. My mother doesn't enjoy cooking although she has done so for many years. __________
5. I will be happy if I get in to the university of my choice. __________

Task 15

각 문장들이 단순(simple), 중문(compound), 복합문장(complex)인지를 판단하시오. 그리고 나서 각 독립절에 밑줄을 치시오.

Example:

Success on this examination means a lot to me, so I am determined to do well.

(complex) Success on this examination means a lot to me, so I am determined to do well.

(1) (   ) Since the weather was so strange, we weren't able to grow enough fruit.

(2) (   ) We managed to cover the museum, the park, and the shopping district all in one day.

(3) (   ) He only smokes while he is drinking with his buddies from home.

(4) (   ) My wife likes to read, while I prefer television.

Task 16

모든 불완전한 문장들을 완전한 문장으로 만드시오.

(1) When he calls you tonight.

(2) Since I love you so much.

(3) Last night after we met.

(4) Wherever she goes, she's happy.

(5) Because you never listen.

Unit 12

Expressing Opinions

1. Facts and opinions
2. Transition Signals for opinions
   1) Stating an opinion
      - In my opinion,
      - In my view,
      - From my point of view,
      - I believe / It is my belief (that)
      - I think (that)
      - There is no doubt (that)
   2) Providing information from an outside source
      - According to (sth/sb),
3. Adjective clauses with *who, which*, and *that*

1. 사실과 의견
2. 의견을 나타내는 연결어
   1) 의견 말하기
      - 내 의견으로는,
      - 내 관점으로는,
      - 내 견해로는,
      - 나는 ~라고 믿는다.
      - 나는 ~라고 생각한다.
      - ~에는 의심할 여지가 없다.
   2) 외부 출처로부터의 정보 제공하기
      - ~에 따르면,
3. *who, which*, 그리고 *that*과 함께 쓰이는 형용사절(관계사절)

Task 17

아래의 상자에서 적절한 단어나 표현들을 골라 각 문장들을 완성 시키시오.

exhausted	get it	hit the books
nonstop	impressed	impressive
bring up	deprived	go too far
stuff	well-rounded	working

(1) Jake studies so hard now because he was _____ of an education in his childhood.

(2) We were really _____ by the first part and the end, but the middle wasn't very ___________.

(3) She tried to explain the instructions to me, but I just didn't ________.

(4) It is important to _____ before a big exam, but getting a good night's sleep is also crucial.

(5) Everybody says that the students at that school are the most _________ but, I think our students have just as many activities, skills and interests as them.

Task 18

주어진 부분을 읽고, 여러분의 의견을 써서 문장을 완성하시오.

1. In my view, plastic surgery ___________________________.

2. I believe that walking _________________________________.

3. In my opinion ________________________________.

4. I think that ____________________________.

5. According to__________, ____________________.

Task 19

아래 주제에 대한 의견을 쓰세요. 모든 문장에 연결어를 사용하시오.

1. Topic: Plastic Surgery

    Opinion:____.

    Support:________________________________. (fact/opinion)

    Support:________________________________. (fact/opinion)

2. Topic: Hagwons in Korea

    Opinion:____.

    Support:________________________________. (fact/opinion)

    Support:________________________________. (fact/opinion)

3. Topic: Blind Dates

    Opinion:____.

    Support:________________________________. (fact/opinion)

    Support:________________________________. (fact/opinion)

Task 20

다음 빈칸에 'who' 또는 'which'를 넣어 각 문장을 완성하시오.

(1) In the event of trouble please contact the Help Desk, _____ is located in the Administrative Office.

(2) I fell in love with one of my coworkers, _____ really confused my parents.

(3) The decision will be made by the committee, _____ is a group of people elected by the shareholders.

(4) You should think carefully about choosing your advisor, _____ is the one that will help you the most.

(5) The referee from last night's game, _____ made several bad calls, was attacked this morning.

Answers & Translation

Unit 1

Comprehension questions

Answers:

1. (a) 2. (c) 3. (d)

Translation:

1. Katherine은 어디서 태어났습니까?
   a) 광주 b) 뉴욕 c) 텍사스 d) 플로리다

2. 왜 Fred는 놀랐습니까?
   a) 그가 매우 일찍 왔기 때문에
   b) 그가 한국에 오랫동안 있지 않았기 때문에
   c) 그가 Katherine이 미국인인 것을 몰랐기 때문에
   d) 그는 Katherine이 그의 상관인걸 몰랐었기 때문에

3. Fred는 언제 한국에 도착하였습니까?
   a) 2일 전에 b) 2시간 전에
   c) 3일 전에 d) 3시간 전에

Task 1

Answers:

- Kind, average-height, was a stay-at-home mom. ( )
- Now she works at a clothing store ( )
- 50 years old, born on July 1, 1961 ( )
- Lives in Busan with my father, born in Changwon Province ( )
- Grew up in the countryside, grew up poor ( )
- Helped on the family farm. Picked crops with her brother ( )

- Her grandmother passed away when she was in high school. She was kind.
(V)
- Her brother became a businessman. He works for Samsung. (V)
- He has two children (V)
- I want my mother and father to move to Seoul. (V)
- Patient. Never scolded me when I did poorly at school ( )
- My father was very strict. (V)
- Liked to play the piano. Taught me when I was little ( )
- On the weekends, she hikes, shops, and spends time with friends. ( )
- Sometimes, she visits me and my brother. ( )
- She takes care of my father. ( )
- Soon he will retire. He wants to travel one day. (V)

Translation:

- 친절한, 보통 키, 주부 ( )
- 지금 그녀는 옷 가게에서 일한다. ( )
- 50세, 1961년 7월 1일 태어나셨다. ( )
- 부산에서 아버지와 함께 사신다. ( )
- 창원지역에서 태어나셨다. ( )
- 시골에서 가난하게 자라셨다. ( )
- 가족의 농사일을 도우셨다. 그녀의 남동생과 곡물을 키우셨다. ( )
- 그녀의 할머니는 그녀가 고등학생 때 돌아가셨다 그녀는 친절했다. (V)
- 그녀의 남동생은 회사원이 되었다. 그는 삼성에서 일한다. (V)
- 그에게는 두 명의 자녀가 있다. (V)
- 나는 어머니와 아버지가 서울로 이사오시기를 바란다. (V)
- 인내심이 있으시다. 내가 학교에서 공부를 잘 못할 때에도 절대 꾸짖지 않으신다.
( )
- 나의 아버지는 매우 엄격했다. (V)
- 그녀는 피아노 치는 것을 좋아했다. 내가 어렸을 때 나에게 가르쳐 주기도 하셨다.
( )
- 주말에 그녀는 등산, 쇼핑, 그리고 친구들을 만난다. ( )
- 때때루 그녀는 나와 내 남동생을 보러 오신다. ( )
- 그녀는 아버지를 잘 돌본다. ( )
- 그는 곧 은퇴하게 된다. 그는 언젠가는 여행을 떠나고 싶어하신다. (V)

Task 2

Answers:

2.

> Grew up in the countryside, grew up poor
> Helped on the family farm.
> Picked crops with her brother and grandmother.

3.

> Kind, average-height was a stay-at-home mom
> Patient. Never scolded me when I did poorly at school.
> Liked to play the piano. Taught me when I was little.

4.

> Now she works at a clothing store
> On the weekends, she hikes, shops, and spends time with friends.
> Sometimes, she visits me and my brother.
> She takes care of my father.

Task 3

Answers:

1. F (no verb)
2. S
3. F (no subject)
4. F (no verb, incomplete thought)
5. F (no object, incomplete thought)

6. S (The subject in this sentence is "you.")

Translation:

1. Long Island 출신의 우리 선생님
2. 그는 방금 한국에 도착했습니다.
3. 매우 큽니다
4. Katherine과 세 명의 여형제들
5. 그녀는 좋아합니다
6. 서둘러라!

Task 4

Translation:

1. 당신의 이름은 무엇입니까?
2. 당신은 언제, 어디에서 태어났습니까?
3. 당신의 가족은 몇 명입니까?
4. 당신은 성격은 어떻습니까?
5. 당신의 여가시간에 무엇을 하기를 좋아합니까?
6. 당신은 왜 CUFS에서 공부합니까?
7. 당신은 미래에 무엇을 하기를 원합니까?

Sample answers:

My name is Frederick Ulysses Morgan, but most people call me Fred. I was born in the year 1976 in Long Island, New York. I have three brothers and two sisters, so including myself there are eight people in my family. I am an enthusiastic and curious person, but sometimes I am a little clumsy and forgetful. In my free time I like to play the guitar, ride my bicycle, and hang out with my friends. I am teaching in Korea because I want to learn about Korean culture and meet many new people. In the future I want to travel all over the world.

나의 이름은 Frederick Ulysses Morgan입니다. 하지만 대부분 사람들은 Fred라 부릅니다. 나는 1976년에 뉴욕의 롱 아일랜드에서 태어났습니다. 나는 세 명의 남자형제와 두 명의 여자형제가 있습니다. 그래서 나는 나를 포함하여 여덟 명의 가족이 있습니다. 나는 열정적이고 호기심 많은 사람입니다. 하지만 때때로 나는 약간 어설프게 일을 하거나 무언가를 잊어버립니다. 나의 여가 시간에 기타연주를 하거나, 자전거를 타거나, 나의 친구들 만나기를 좋아합니다. 나는 한국에서 학생들을 가르칩니다. 왜냐하면 나는 한국문화에 대해서 배우길 원하고, 많은 새로운 사람들을 만나기를 원하기 때문입니다. 미래에 나는 전 세계를 여행하기를 원합니다.

Unit 2

Task 1

Answers:

(1) poor me (2) go to school
(3) is self-conscious about (4) myself
(5) go home

Translation:

오, 한심스러워요! 저는 매일 학교에 갈 때, 제 얼굴에는 항상 몇 개의 여드름이 있습니다. 모든 사람들은 자신의 얼굴에 콤플렉스를 가지고 있기 때문에 이것은 중요합니다. 제 자신에 대한 신뢰를 잃게 될 때, 학교생활도 끔찍하게 느껴집니다. 그리고 나서 집으로 간 후 내 방에 가서 오랫동안 웁니다. 이것은 제가 걱정하는 유일한 것은 아니지만, 가장 큰 문제입니다.

Task 2

Answers:

1. (3) 2. (4) 3. (1)
4. (3) 5. (3) 6. (1)

Translation:

예: 나의 할머니는 체스 두는 것을 무척 좋아하시고 나와 놀아주십니다.

1. 나의 할머니는 80세가 넘으셨다 하지만 연세에 비해 아주 활동적이십니다.
2. 그녀와 나의 할아버지는 70년이 넘게 서로를 알고 지내셨고 결혼해서 사신지 60년이 되었습니다.
3. 그들은 3명의 자녀, 5명의 손주와 4명의 증손을 두었습니다.
4. 나의 할머니는 파티를 좋아하시고 한 달에 한 번씩 온 가족을 초대하여 저녁식사를 합니다.
5. 이러한 가족모임 때 그녀는 우리를 위해 요리를 하고 케이크와 쿠키를 만들어 주시기도 합니다.
6. 그녀는 거의 밤새 주무시지 않고 이야기를 하여도 피곤해하지 않으십니다.

Task 3

Answers:

1. SV: My dog sleeps on the floor next to my bed. / My dog sleeps next to my bed on the floor.
2. SVV: We don't have school or take Taekwondo lessons on Mondays. / We don't take Taekwondo lessons or have school on Mondays.
3. SSVV: My sister and I would like to fly to Hawaii and walk on the beaches.

Translation:

예: 나의 형은 대학에 가서 아르바이트를 합니다.

1. SV : 나의 강아지는 내 침대 옆 바닥에서 잡니다.
2. SVV : 월요일에 우리는 학교에 가지 않고 태권도 수업도 받지 않습니다.
3. SSVV : 언니와 저는 하와이에 가서 해변을 걷고 싶습니다.

Task 4

Answers:

1. Bora can speak and understand Japanese.
2. Jimin can't speak Chinese or Thai.
3. Green and white are my favorite colors.
4. Her English is strongly accented but intelligible.
5. I might have beer, wine, or juice.

Translation:

1. 보라는 일본어로 말할 수 있고, 이해할 수 있습니다.
2. 지민은 중국어 또는 태국어로 말할 수 없습니다.
3. 초록색과 흰색은 내가 좋아하는 색깔이다.
4. 그녀의 영어에는 외국인 엑센트가 강하게 들리지만 알아들을 수 있습니다.
5. 저는 아마 맥주, 와인 또는 주스를 마실 겁니다.

Task 5

Answers:

1. How long have you been in Korea?

2. Help, I am being robbed!
3. Korea has four seasons.
4. You've been to New York before, haven't you?
5. Call an ambulance!
6. She asked me where to go.
7. Oh no, he's got a gun!

Translation:

1. 당신은 얼마나 한국에 있었나요?
2. 도와주세요, 강도예요!
3. 한국에는 사계절이 있습니다.
4. 당신은 전에 뉴욕에 가본적이 있죠?
5. 구급차를 불러주세요!
6. 그녀는 내게 어디로 갈 지 물었습니다.
7. 안돼요, 그는 총을 가지고 있어요!

Task 6

Answers:

1. My　　2. I　　3. Scottish
4. Celtic　　5. Bum-Kun (or Bum-kun, or Bumnkun),
6. Asian　　7. FIFA

Translation:

제 이름은 차두리입니다. 그리고 저는 흥미진진한 인생을 살아왔습니다. 저는 스코틀랜드 프리미어 리그 셀틱 클럽의 직업 축구선수입니다. 저의 아버지 차범근은 1986년 월드컵에서 경기를 했습니다. 그리고 저는 2010년에 경기했습니다. 그것은 제가 한국에서 그리고 아시아에서 제 2세대 선수로서 FIFA월드컵에서 경기한 첫 번째 선수임을 의미합니다. 저는 세계무대에서 우리나라를 대표하는 것을 자랑스럽게 생각했습니다.

Unit 3

Comprehension questions

Answers:

1. (a) 2. (d) 3. (b)

Translation:

1. Katherine의 일과를 순서대로 쓴 것은?
   a) 조깅 → 수업 → 점심→ 한국어수업
   b) 수업 → 한국어수업 → 점심 → 조깅
   c) 점심 → 수업 → 조깅 → 한국어수업
   d) 한국어수업 → 점심 → 조깅 → 수업

2. Fred의 활동 중 하나가 아닌 것은?
   a) 식사 b) 사교활동 c) 관광 d) 자원봉사

3. Katherine과 Fred가 말이 암시하는 것은?
   a) 미국인은 목욕을 하지 않는다.
   b) 미국인들은 목욕을 하기 전에 샤워를 하지 않는다.
   c) 미국인들은 아침에 샤워를 하고, 저녁에는 하지 않는다.
   d) 미국인들은 한국인보다 지저분하다.

Task 1

Answers:

1. (b) 2. (a&c) 3. (d)

Translation:

1. 다음 중 "수업을 선택하는 방법"에 대해 도리가 쓴 단락에 포함되어야 하는 아이디어는 어떤 것입니까?
   a) 대학에 다니는 동안 즐겨라.
   b) 학과 코스 목록과 당신 전공의 필수 조건에 대해서 읽어라.
   c) 가능한 많은 책을 읽어라.
   d) 올바른 사람을 선택하기 위해서 시간을 보내라.

2. 다음 중 같은 것을 의미하는 두 개를 고르시오.
   a) 선수 과목
   b) 숙제
   c) 먼저 수강했어야 하는 과목
   d) 계획을 많이 세워라.

3. 선배들에게 수업에 대해서 물어봄으로써 학생들은 무엇을 배울 수 있습니까?
   a) 그 수업들이 좋은지
   b) 그 수업들이 나쁜지
   c) 그들이 졸업을 해야만 하는지
   d) a와 b 모두

Task 2

Answers:

(e, f & k)

Translation:

a. 졸업에 필요한 수업을 알아보십시오.
b. 매 학기 들어야 할 수업의 목록을 만드십시오.
c. 학과 코스 목록과 전공 필수조건을 읽으십시오.
d. 일찍 수강신청을 하십시오.
e. 아르바이트를 하십시오.
f. 헌책방에 대해서 알아보십시오.

g. 선수 과목에 대해서 알아보십시오.

h. 수업에 대한 조언을 얻기 위해 고학년 학생들과 얘기를 나누십시오.

i. 어떤 수업이 괜찮나요?

j. 어떤 수업이 나쁜가요?

k. 많이 즐기십시오.

Task 3

Answers:

d

Translation:

A. 많은 계획을 세우십시오.

B. 가능한 많은 선배들과 이야기를 나누십시오

C. 전공의 졸업 요건에 익숙해지십시오.

D. 가능한 빨리 각 과목의 수강신청을 하십시오.

Task 4

Answers:

My Dad, the Music Fan

My Dad is a music fan. His favorite genres of music are ballads(,) rock(,) and hip hop. He listens to rock songs in the morning(,) sings ballads in the afternoon(,) and practices hip hop dancing in the evening. He also watches concerts and dance competitions on TV. Our living room looks like a karaoke room(,) and his bedroom looks like a dance studio. There are guitars(,) drums(,) microphones(,) and CDs all around the house. Sometimes I wonder if my father is a businessman or a pop idol.

Translation:

나의 아버지, 음악 팬

나의 아버지는 음악 팬입니다. 좋아하는 음악장르는 발라드, 록, 그리고 힙합입니다. 그는 아침에 록음악을 듣고, 점심에는 발라드를 부릅니다. 그리고 저녁에는 힙합 춤을 연습합니다. 그는 또한 TV로 콘서트와 댄스 대회를 봅니다. 우리의 거실은 가라오케 방 같고, 그리고 그의 침실은 댄스 스튜디오 같습니다. 온 집안에 기타, 드럼, 마이크, 그리고 CD가 있습니다. 가끔씩 나는 아버지가 사업가인지 팝 아이 돌인지 궁금합니다.

Task 5

Answers:

1. I've studied math, science, and literature.
2. I'd like to go to Tokyo, Paris, and Egypt.
3. When you travel to a different city or country, be sure to take money, a credit card, your passport, enough socks and underwear, and common sense.
4. My hobbies are hiking and reading. (Remember: no comma in lists with only two items.)
5. Every weekend, I visit my grandmother, watch TV, and call my parents.

Translation:

예: 당신이 좋아하는 세 가지 음식을 알려주는 문장을 쓰시오.
나는 한국 김치, 멕시코 타코, 그리고 프랑스 크로와상을 좋아합니다.

1. 나는 수학, 과학, 문학을 공부했습니다.
2. 나는 도쿄, 파리, 이집트에 가고 싶어요.
3. 다른 도시 또는 국가를 여행하는 경우, 돈, 신용 카드, 여권, 충분한 양말, 속옷, 휴대폰, 그리고 상식이 꼭 필요합니다.
4. 내 취미는 등산과 독서 입니다. (주의: 목록에 두 항목만 있으면 쉼표생략.)
5. 매 주말, 나는 나의 할머니를 방문하고, TV를 시청하고, 부모님께 전화합니다.

Unit 4

Task 1

Answers:

(1) to help (2) While (3) in front of my
(4) After that (5) dress (6) but if
(7) as much as possible / as much as I can

Translation:

나의 일상

아침에 일어나서 내가 제일먼저 하는 일은 나의 잠을 깰 수 있게 도와주는 커피를 만드는 일이다. 커피가 만들어지는 동안 나는 냉동된 딸기 한 그릇을 쏟아 붓고 그것들이 해동되기를 기다린다. 나는 주로 나의 이메일을 확인하는 동안 내 컴퓨터 앞에서 아침을 먹는다. 그 후에 샤워를 하고 머리를 다듬는다. 그리고 나서 나는 출근을 하기 위해 옷을 고르는데, 주로 편안한 옷을 고른다. 시간이 여유로운 날에는 나는 전철을 타고 출근한다. 그러나 늦을 것 같으면 대신 택시를 탄다. 나는 8시간 동안 일을 하고 집으로 돌아온다. 내가 기운이 있으면, 조깅을 하거나 자전거를 탄다. 그리고 난 후 나는 저녁을 만들고, 영어 공부를 되도록 많이 하고 잠자리에 든다.

Task 2

Answers:

1. S 2. C 3. S 4. S
5. C 6. S 7. S

Translation:

1. 어제 나는 내 방을 청소하고 강아지를 산책시켰습니다.
2. 오늘밤에 우리는 영화를 보고 싶지만, 어떤 것을 봐야 할지 모르겠습니다.
3. 남동생과 나는 아주 친한 사이입니다.
4. 그녀는 쇼핑을 갔지만 계란과 야채를 구입하는 것을 잊어버렸습니다.
5. 오늘은 비가 내립니다. 그래서 우리는 빨래를 할 수 없습니다.
6. 나의 선생님과 그의 가족은 버섯이나 조개를 좋아하지 않습니다.
7. 저녁 식사 후 우리는 뮤지컬을 보러 가거나 노래방에 갈 수 있습니다.

Task 3

Answers:

1. Hong-cheol brought the cake, and Jae-seok brought the ice cream.
2. G-Dragon and T.O.P. had a fight, so the concert was cancelled.
3. Soo-young is tall, but Sunny is short.
4. I was late to class, so my teacher punished me.
5. Last night Dad made dinner, and/so Mom washed the dishes.
6. We have to hurry or we will be late for the train.
7. I wanted to wake up early this morning, but I forgot to set my alarm.

Translation:

1. 홍철이는 케이크를 가지고 사왔고 재석이는 아이스크림을 가지고 사왔습니다.
2. G-드래곤과 탑은 싸웠습니다. 그래서 공연이 취소되었습니다.
3. 수영은 키가 크지만 써니는 작습니다.
4. 나는 수업에 늦었습니다. 그래서 선생님은 내게 벌을 주셨습니다.
5. 어제 밤에 아빠가 저녁 식사를 만들었습니다. 그리고 / 그래서 엄마가 설거지를 했습니다.
6. 우리는 서둘러야 합니다. 그렇지 않으면 우리는 기차시간에 늦을 것입니다.
7. 나는 오늘 아침 일찍 일어났습니다. 하지만, 나의 알람을 설정하는 것을 잊어버렸습니다.

Task 4

Answers:

1. Barack Obama resides at 1600 Pennsylvania Avenue, Washington, D.C. (또는 Washington D.C.)
2. The World Trade Center in New York was attacked on September 11, 2011.
3. More than 700,000,000 species of animal life have been found in that region alone.
4. Last year, her annual salary was increased from $59,560.50 to $61,345.
5. The percentage of change amounted to exactly 0.28456 degrees. (no commas)
6. Dear Mr. Gates: I am writing to offer a business proposition... (colon, not comma)
7. Dear Grandma, Thank you so much for the birthday gift...

Translation:

1. Barak Obama는, 워싱턴, D.C.에 있는 Pennsylvania Avenue 1600번지에 거주합니다.
2. 뉴욕에 있는 세계무역센터는 2011년 9월 11일에 공격을 받았습니다.
3. 7억 종이 넘는 동물들의 생태가 그 지역에서만 발견되었습니다.
4. 작년에 그녀의 연봉은 5만 9천 569 달러에서 6만 1천 345달러로 인상되었습니다.
5. 변화율은 정확하게 0.28456도에 도달하였습니다.
6. Gates씨에게: 사업상 제의를 제안하기 위해 편지를 씁니다.
7. 할머니께, 생일 선물 정말 감사합니다.

Task 5

Answers:

1. Her parents live in Los Angeles, California but they have a small vacation home in Boulder, Colorado.
2. According to my friend's uncle, aliens visited Earth about 250,000 years ago.
3. Please note that all letters sent to our office at 17 Fulton Street, Brooklyn will be forwarded to the main headquarters at 1800 Seventh Avenue, Manhattan.
4. Olivia woke up, took a shower, got dressed, and went to school.
5. Because my mother works so hard during the day, she never has any energy in the evening.
6. I fell asleep during the exam yesterday, but nobody woke me up.
7. New York is predicted to have over 9,000,000 people by the year 2015.

Translation:

1. 그녀의 부모님은 California주에 있는 Los Angeles에 사시지만, Colorado 주에 있는 Boulder에 작은 별장을 가지고 있습니다.
2. 내 친구의 삼촌에 따르면, 외계인들은 약 25만년 전에 지구에 방문했었다고 합니다.
3. 우리 사무실 주소인 17 Fulton Street, Brooklyn 로 보내온 모든 편지는 본사인 1800 Seventh Avenue, Manhattan으로 전달될 수 있도록 해주십시오.
4. Olivia는 일어나서, 샤워를 하고, 옷을 입고 난 후 학교에 갔습니다.
5. 저의 어머니는 낮 동안 열심히 일을 하시기 때문에, 저녁에는 늘 기운이 없습니다.
6. 어제 시험을 보는 동안에 잠이 들었지만, 아무도 날 깨우지 않았습니다.
7. 뉴욕에서 2015년이 되면 9백만 명이 넘는 사람이 살게 될 것이라고 예측됩니다.

Unit 5

Comprehension questions

Answers:

1. (3)　　2. (2)　　3. (1)

Translation:

1. Fred는 주말에 무엇을 했나요?
   (1) 집에 있었다.
   (2) 김치를 만들었다.
   (3) 민호네 집에 갔다.
   (4) 멋진 휴가를 보냈다.

2. Fred가 민호의 집에 들어 갔을 때 잊은 것은 무엇인가요?
   (1) 신발을 계속 신고 있는 것
   (2) 신발 벗는 것
   (3) 김치를 사오는 것
   (4) 김치를 냉장고에 넣는 것

3. Katherine 과 Fred가 점심시간에 무엇에 관해 이야기하기로 했나요?
   (1) Katherine의 휴가
   (2) Fred의 휴가
   (3) Katherine의 홈스테이
   (4) Fred의 홈스테이

Task 1

Answers:

1. sofa and cushions　　2. window

3. TV
4. sliding door 1
5. fireplace
6. sliding door 2
7. armrest chair and cushions
8. coffee table

Translation:

1. 소파와 쿠션
2. 창문
3. 텔레비전
4. 미닫이 문 1
5. 벽난로
6. 미닫이 문 2
7. 팔걸이가 있는 의자와 쿠션
8. 커피 테이블

Task 2

Answers:

1. b
2. d
3. b

Translation:

1. 이 상황이 일어나고 있는 곳은 어디인가요?
   a. 해변
   b. 공원
   c. 누군가의 정원
   d. 위 모두 정답이 아닙니다.

2. 다음 중 위 그림 속의 인물을 묘사하는 것이 아닌 것은?
   a. 산책을 하고 있는 가족
   b. 의자에 앉아 있는 커플
   c. 자전거를 타고 있는 남자
   d. 길을 따라 달리고 있는 개들

3. 다음 중 위 그림을 가장 잘 묘사한 것은?
   a. 햇살이 공원을 비추고 있습니다. 호수에는 많은 동물이 있습니다.
   b. 사람들이 붐비는 일요일의 공원입니다. 한 남자가 자전거를 타고 있고, 한 가족은 산책을 하고 있습니다. 세 명의 조깅하는 사람들이 벤치에 앉아 산을 바라보고 있는 커플을 지나치고 있습니다.
   c. 공원에서 자전거를 타고 있는 남자가 한 명 있습니다. 그리고 여러 가족들과 조깅을 하는 사람들이 있습니다. 또한 한 커플이 벤치에 앉아있습니다. 공원이 있습니다.
   d. 위 모두 정답이 아닙니다.

Task 3

Answers:

The woman in the picture is young. She has long black hair. Her face is small, and her features are symmetrical. She is wearing a pale pink ruffled blouse.

Translation:

사진 속의 여자는 젊습니다. 긴 검정색 머리를 가지고 있어요. 얼굴은 작고 이목구비는 균형을 이루고 있습니다. 그리고 그녀는 옅은 분홍색의 주름장식이 달린 블라우스를 입고 있습니다.

Task 4

Answers:

1. apartment: first, small, dark, ugly
2. building: dirty, old
3. kitchen: tiny, greasy, disgusting
4. bathroom: smelly, wet
5. furniture: stinky, used

6. bedroom: little, pink
7. room: windowless, quiet, boring, peaceful, relaxing

Translation:

예: The last meal I ate was expensive and delicious.
meal: last, expensive, delicious
내가 먹은 지난번 식사는 비쌌고 맛있었습니다.

나의 첫 번째 아파트

나의 첫 번째 아파트는 작고, 어둡고 형편 없었습니다. 그것은 Brooklyn 에 위치한 지저분한 오래된 건물의 비좁고 두 개의 방으로 된 아파트였습니다. 작은 부엌은 기름투성이에 지저분했으며, 냄새 나는 욕실은 항상 축축했고, 곰팡이로 가득했습니다. 그 중 최악은 쥐가 우글거리는 거실이었습니다. 거실은 항상 악취가 풍기는 중고 가구로 넘쳐났으며 아무리 치워도 항상 먼지투성이였습니다. 내가 제일 좋아했던 장소는 분홍색의 작은 침실이었습니다. 창문이 없는 침실은 조용했고 따분했으나, 그와 동시에 평화로웠고 안락함을 주었습니다. 멋진 곳으로 생각되지 않을 것입니다. 그러나 어쨌든 그 곳은 내 집이었고, 난 그곳을 사랑했습니다.

Task 5

Answers:

My Car

The outside **of** my car is always clean and shiny, but the inside **of** my car is always a mess. **On** the driver's seat there is a lot of pocket change, and **in** the passenger's seat are many magazines. Receipts are scattered **across** the dashboard, while the floor **of** the front seat is filled **with** trash. That sounds bad, but the area **behind** the front seats is even worse! The only tidy spot **in** the back is the baby seat. **Next to** the baby seat is a huge teddy bear named Edward, and the space **between** Edward and the door is completely stuffed **with** toys **of** all shapes and sizes. I have absolutely no idea what is **beneath** the seats. Sometimes I think it might be easier to buy a new car than to clean this one!

Translation:

예: The tallest building (in) the world is (in) Dubai.
세상에서 가장 높은 건물은 두바이에 있습니다.

나의 차

내 차의 외관은 항상 깨끗하고 빛이 나지만, 내 차의 내부는 항상 지저분합니다. 운전석에는 많은 잔돈이 있고, 조수석에는 많은 잡지가 있습니다. 영수증이 계기판 주위에 흩어져있고 앞자리의 바닥에는 쓰레기로 가득합니다. 이것만 해도 이미 지저분하게 들리겠지만, 앞 좌석 뒤의 공간은 훨씬 더합니다. 뒷자리에서 유일하게 깔끔한 공간은 아기용 좌석입니다. 아기 좌석 옆으로는, Edward라는 이름을 가진 커다란 곰 인형이 있고, Edward와 문 사이 공간은 완전히 온갖 종류와 다양한 크기의 장난감들로 가득합니다. 나는 좌석 아랫부분에 어떤 것들이 있는지 전혀 짐작이 가지 않습니다. 가끔 나는 이 차를 청소 하는 것보다, 새 차를 하나 사는 것이 더 쉽겠다고 생각합니다.

Unit 6

Task 1

Answers:

(1) went
(2) from which
(3) the daytime
(4) the low humidity
(5) who live

Translation:

완벽한 휴가지

나는 하와이에 15년 전에 갔었고, 지금까지도 그 여행에 있어서 좋은 기억을 가지고 있습니다. 하와이에서 다시 한번 휴가를 보내고 싶습니다. 나는 바다가 보이는 호텔의 방을 얻을 것이다. 야자나무, 깨끗한 공기, 그리고 맑은 물이 있습니다. 따뜻한 편이고 낮에는 약간 덥습니다. 그러나, 습도가 낮아서 집안에 있으며 그리 덥게 느껴지지 않고 밤에는 서늘합니다. 그곳에 사는 사람들은 밝고 친절해 보인다. 그들은 느긋하고 여유가 있어서, 그들을 만나는 일은 즐겁습니다.

Task 2

Answers:

1. In the center of the yard
2. from the fountain, onto some rocks around it
3. Under the trees
4. Near the fountain
5. After lunch, in the cafeteria

Translation:

1. 뜰 가운데 분수가 있습니다.
2. 물이 분수로부터 그 근처 바위들로 튑니다.
3. 나무 아래 나무로 만들어진 벤치와 테이블이 있습니다.
4. 분수 근처에 키 큰 삼나무들이 있습니다.
5. 점심시간이 지나면 카페테리아 안은 조용합니다.

Task 3

Sample answers:

1. The Waikiki Sunrise Hotel is next to the beach.
   Next to the beach is the Waikiki Sunrise Hotel.
2. Four rooms are inside each suite: a master bedroom, a bathroom, a living room, and an entertainment room.
   Inside each suite are four rooms: a master bedroom, a bathroom, a

living room, and an entertainment room.

3. There is a luxurious Jacuzzi in every bathroom.
   In every bathroom, there is a luxurious Jacuzzi.
4. A beautiful, sunny veranda is outside every living room.
   Outside every living room is a beautiful, sunny veranda.
5. There are restaurants, cafes, and luxury boutiques on the first floor of the hotel.
   On the first floor of the hotel, there are restaurants, cafes, and luxury boutiques.
6. The hotel staff will escort you to your room upon your arrival.
   Upon your arrival, the hotel staff will escort you to your room.
7. You will be treated like kings and queens until your departure.
   Until your departure, you will be treated like kings and queens.

Translation:

1. Waikiki Sunrise Hotel은 바닷가 옆에 있습니다.
2. 모든 스위트 룸에는 네 개의 방이 있습니다: 안방, 욕실, 거실, 그리고 휴게실.
3. 욕실마다 화려한 기포가 생기는 욕조 자쿠찌가 있습니다.
4. 모든 거실 밖으로는 예쁘고 햇살이 비치는 베란다가 있습니다.
5. 호텔 일층에는 레스토랑, 카페, 그리고 화려한 상점들이 있습니다.
6. 도착하자마자 호텔 직원은 당신을 방으로 안내할 것입니다.
7. 호텔을 나설 때까지 당신은 귀빈 대접을 받을 것입니다.

Task 4

Answers:

1. The limousine will be waiting for you outside the airport.
2. We saw a beautiful rainbow above the waterfall.
3. You are not allowed to smoke inside the plane.
4. The grocery store is located between the post office and the bank.
5. Since there were guards all around the building, they had to escape through the sewer.

6. I thought she left her hat on that chair, but it might be under the bed.
7. Please take your laptop out of the bag and place it in the tray.

Task 5

Answers:

1. e	2. c	3. a	4. b
5. d	6. f	7. g	

Translation:

1. 날씨가 너무 더워서 내가 녹는 것 같다.
2. 시험이 너무 어려워서 그 수업을 취소하기로 했다.
3. 집이 너무 커서, 집 안에서 길을 잃을 수도 있을 것 같다.
4. 난 너무 당황해서 어디로든 숨고 싶었다.
5. 그건 너무 재미있는 얘기라서 우리는 웃으면서 바닥에 데굴데굴 굴렀다.
6. 나는 너무 많이 먹어서, 위가 터져버릴 것 같다.
7. Brad가 너무 끔찍한 짓을 저질러서 Angelina는 그를 찼다..

Task 6

Sample answers:

1A: Barcelona is so beautiful that I would like to live there someday.
1B: Barcelona has such confusing streets that I got lost several times.
2A: "The Tourist" was so boring that I fell asleep.
2B: "The Tourist" was such a disappointing movie that I asked for a refund.
3A: My best friend was so friendly that he made new friends every time he went out.
3B: My best friend was such a great guy that everybody loved him.

4A: My college writing class was so stressful that it kept me up at night.
4B: It was such a difficult class that only one student got an A+.

Translation:

(1) 당신이 좋아하는 장소
(2) 당신이 본 영화
(3) 당신이 정말 좋아하는 (혹은 싫어하는) 사람
(4) 당신이 들은 수업

1A: Barcelona가 너무 아름다워서 나는 언젠가 그 곳에서 살고 싶습니다.
1B: Barcelona는 거리가 너무 헷갈리게 되어 있어서 나는 여러 번 길을 잃었습니다.
2A: "여행자" 는 너무 지루해서 나는 잠이 들었습니다.
2B: "여행자" 는 너무 실망스러운 영화여서 나는 환불을 요청했습니다.
3A: 나의 단짝 친구는 너무 다정해서 밖에 나갈 때마다 새로운 친구들을 만들어 옵니다.
3B: 나의 단짝 친구는 너무 멋진 남자라서 모든 사람들이 그를 좋아합니다.
4A: 대학 작문 수업 때문에 너무 스트레스를 받아서 나는 계속 밤을 새워야 했습니다.
4B: 그것은 정말 어려운 수업이었기에 오직 한 학생만이 A+받았습니다.

Unit 7

Task 1

Answers:

1. retires
2. exhausted
3. Let me guess
4. figured/figures, was adopted
5. freshen up

Translation:

1. 나는 곧 우리 아버지께서 은퇴하시길 바랍니다. 그는 점점 나이가 들어가고 있고, 나는 그와 함께 더 많은 시간을 보내고 싶습니다.

2. 우리 어머니는 하루 종일 열심히 일하십니다. 그래서 그녀는 집에 올 때면 항상 지쳐 있습니다.
3. 당신은 매일매일 맥도날드에서 먹습니까? 맞춰볼게요, 당신은 미국인입니다. 맞습니까?
4. 그녀는 내가 입양되었다는 사실을 알아냈습니다. 왜냐하면 나는 우리 부모님과 전혀 닮지 않았기 때문입니다.
5. 나는 하루 종일 버스에 있었습니다. 그래서 외식하러 가기 전에 몸단장을 하고 싶습니다.

Task 2

Answers:

1. title
2. Indent
3. Begin, Don't start / Start, Don't begin
4. Write

Translation:

1. 당신의 문단에 제목을 붙이세요.
2. 당신의 문단의 첫 문장을 대략 1.25 cm 정도 들여쓰기 하세요.
3. 각 문장은 앞 선 문장이 끝나는 지점에서 시작하세요. 각각의 새로운 문장을 새 줄에서 시작해서는 안됩니다.
4. 만약 한 단어가 너무 길어서 한 줄에 맞지 않는다면, 그 다음 줄에 전체 단어를 쓰세요.

Task 3

Sample answers:

Introduction

Competitive swimming provides same benefits as other sports

a. It is good exercise and builds muscular strength
b. It promotes cooperation among team members, especially in relays

Competitive swimming provides some additional benefits

a. Swimming is an important skill that can be used forever

b. There is a reduced risk of injury

c. Each swimmer can easily chart his or her own progress

My personal experience as a competitive swimmer

a. I enjoy working with my coach

b. I've made a lot of friends on the swim team

Conclusion

Translation:

도입

수영경기는 다른 스포츠들과 같은 이점을 제공합니다.

a. 그것은 좋은 운동이고, 근육의 힘을 길러줍니다.

b. 그것은 특히 릴레이 경기 시, 팀 멤버 사이에서 협동심을 길러줍니다.

수영 경기는 몇 가지 추가적인 이점을 제공합니다.

a. 수영은 영원히 사용될 수 있는 중요한 능력입니다.

b. 부상의 위험이 적습니다.

c. 각각의 선수는 그들 자신의 향상된 능력을 쉽게 기록할 수 있습니다.

수영 선수로서의 나의 개인적인 경험

a. 나는 나의 코치와 운동하는 것을 즐거워합니다.

b. 나는 수영 팀에서 많은 친구들을 사귀었습니다.

결론

Task 4

Answers:

1. F (no object)
2. S (object not obligatory)
3. F (no subject or verb)
4. F (only subject, no predicate)
5. S
6. F (only subject with relative clause, no predicate)

Translation:

1. 네, 나는 사랑합니다.
2. 나의 어머니는 (음식을) 드셨습니다.
3. 정말 훌륭하군요!
4. 모든 학생들
5. 들어보세요!
6. 부산에 있는 내가 가장 좋아하는 이모

Task 5

Answers:

1. I am so irresponsible.
2. go to work
3. criticizes me
4. myself
5. go home

Oh, (1) I am so irresponsible! When I (2) go to work every day, I am always late. This looks very bad and my boss (3) criticizes me. This makes me lose confidence in (4) myself, thus I feel terrible at work. Then, after I (5) go home and get stressed out that I may lose my job. This is not the only thing that troubles me, but it is the biggest.

Translation:

오, 난 정말 무책임합니다! 매일 출근할 때, 난 항상 지각을 합니다. 이것은 매우 나쁘게 보이고, 나의 상사는 나를 질책합니다. 이것 때문에 나는 자신감을 잃고, 직장에서 몹시 힘듭니다. 그리고 나서 집에 간 후 난 내가 직업을 잃을지도 모른다는 사실에 스트레스를 받습니다. 이것이 나를 괴롭히는 유일한 것은 아니지만, 가장 큰 문제입니다.

Task 6

Answers:

1. and
2. but
3. and
4. or
5. but
6. or

Translation:

1. 수영과 보트 타기는 내가 가장 좋아하는 여름 활동 입니다.
2. 그녀는 그녀의 직업을 좋아하지만, 그녀의 상사는 싫어합니다.
3. 그는 월요일, 수요일 그리고 금요일에 수업이 있습니다.
4. 그들은 소고기 또는 닭고기를 다 좋아하지 않습니다.
5. 나의 부모님은 매우 나이가 드셨지만, 여전히 힘이 넘치십니다.
6. 그는 테니스, 승마 또는 스케이트를 잘 타지 못합니다.

Task 7

Answers:

1. (?) 2. (.) 3. (.) 4. (!) 5. (?)

Translation:

1. 저것은 잘못된 답이 아닌가요?
2. 나는 한번도 프랑스에 가 본적이 없습니다.
3. 내가 말하려고 하는 건, 당신을 사랑한다는 것입니다.
4. 조심하세요, 차가 오고 있습니다.
5. 그녀는 또 늦지 않습니다. 그렇죠?

Task 8

Answers:

1. American
2. TV
3. Fringe
4. It
5. FBI
6. Olivia

Yesterday I watched an American TV show called Fringe. It is about a special FBI team that investigates strange things in the world. I like the main character Olivia, but I think the old scientist is a little strange.

Translation:

어제 나는 'Fringe' 라고 하는 미국 TV 쇼를 보았습니다. 그것은 세상의 이상한 일들을 조사하는 특수 FBI 팀에 관한 것입니다. 나는 주인공인 Olivia는 좋아하는데, 그 나이든 과학자는 조금 이상하다고 생각합니다.

Task 9

Answers:

1. head
2. stuff
3. pretty much
4. kind of
5. grab

Translation:

1. 만약 당신이 준비가 되었다면, 지금 영화관으로 갑시다.
2. 내 책상엔 물건들이 너무 많아서 나는 그 티켓들을 찾을 수가 없습니다.
3. 나는 그 프로젝트를 거의 끝냈습니다. 그러니 우린 곧 떠날 수 있습니다.

4. 액션 영화도 때로 약간 흥미롭지만, 나는 사랑 이야기들을 정말 더 좋아합니다.
5. 영화 시작 전에 우리 팝콘을 사 먹을까요?

Task 10

Sample answers:

- go to class
- review homework
- have lunch with peers
- study at the library
- borrow books from the library
- attend seminars
- walk around campus
- go to the department office
- attend lectures
- go to events
- read on the lawn

Translation:

- 수업 들어가기
- 숙제 복습하기
- 친구들과 점심 먹기
- 도서관에서 공부하기
- 도서관에서 책 빌리기
- 세미나 참석하기
- 캠퍼스 돌아다니기
- 학과 사무실 가기
- 강의 듣기
- 행사 가기
- 잔디밭에서 책 읽기

Task 11

Answers:

(d, g, h)

Translation:

a. 수업 들어가기
b. 숙제 복습하기
c. 친구들과 점심 먹기
d. 최신 할리우드 영화 보기
e. 도서관에서 공부하기
f. 세미나 참석하기
g. 고급 레스토랑에서 식사하기
h. 새 애완동물 구입하기
i. 캠퍼스 돌아다니기
j. 학과 사무실 가기
k. 강의 듣기
l. 행사 가기
m. 잔디밭에서 책 읽기

Task 12

Answers:

When James was a young man**,** he used to love sports. Although he liked all kinds of physical activity**,** his favorite sports were baseball**,** hockey**,** and basketball. He played baseball in the spring and summer**,** hockey in the winter**,** and basketball all year round.

Translation:

제임스가 젊었을 때, 그는 스포츠를 좋아했습니다. 비록 그가 모든 종류의 신체적 활동을 좋아하긴 했지만, 그가 가장 좋아하는 운동은 야구, 하키 그리고 농구였습니다. 그는 봄과 여름에는 야구를 했고, 겨울에는 하키를, 그리고 일년 내내 농구를 했습니다.

Task 13

Answers:

1. Class begins at 3:00 sharp, <u>and the exam will start at 3:10</u>.
2. You have to study hard, <u>or you will fail the test</u>.
3. My sister loves to travel, <u>but she doesn't like to fly</u>.
4. It rained yesterday, <u>so the picnic was cancelled</u>.
5. I really wanted to see the game, <u>but it was sold out</u>.

Translation:

1. 수업은 정확히 3시에 시작을 하고 시험은 3시 10분에 시작 할 것입니다.
2. 당신은 열심히 공부해야만 합니다 그렇지 않으면 시험을 망칠 것입니다.
3. 나의 여동생은 여행하기를 좋아하지만 그녀는 비행기 타는 것을 좋아하지는 않습니다.
4. 어제는 비가 왔었습니다. 그래서 소풍이 취소되었습니다.
5. 나는 정말 그 게임이 보고 싶었지만, 그것은 매진되었습니다.

Task 14

Answers:

1. S 2. C 3. S 4. S 5. C

Translation:

1. 어제 나는 침대 정리를 했고, 강아지를 산책 시켰다.
2. 우리는 불꽃놀이를 보러 가고 싶지만 우리가 제 시간에 갈 수 있을지는 확신할 수 없습니다.
3. 나와 내 여동생은 매우 가깝습니다.
4. 그녀는 쇼핑을 갔지만 토마토와 햄을 사는 것을 잊었습니다.
5. 오늘은 비가 오고 있습니다. 그래서 우리는 야외 소풍을 갈 수 없습니다.

Task 15

Sample answers:

1. Two of my favorite foods are kimchi stew and fried rice.
2. Four movies I like are Gone with the wind, Titanic, Steel Magnolias, and Pretty woman.
3. The three biggest cities in Korea are Seoul, Incheon, and Busan.

Translation:

예: 내가 존경하는 세 명의 사람들은 나의 어머니, 아버지 그리고 스티브 잡스 입니다.

1. 내가 가장 좋아하는 음식 중 두 가지는 김치찌개와 볶음밥입니다.
2. 내가 좋아하는 네 개의 영화는 바람과 함께 사라지다, 타이타닉, 철목련, 그리고 귀여운 여인 입니다.
3. 한국에서 가장 큰 세 도시는 서울, 인천, 그리고 부산입니다.

Task 16

Answers:

1. was like
2. messed up
3. by mistake
4. work out, Anyway
5. makes sense

Translation:

1. 어제 밤 Aliyah는 나에게 전화해서, "Justin의 프레젠테이션은 정말 최악이었어!" 라고 했습니다.
2. 난 당신이 그 프로젝트를 망쳤다는 것을 믿을 수가 없습니다. 도대체 뭐가 문제인건가요?
3. 그가 실수로 잘못된 파일을 가져왔다는 것이 밝혀졌습니다.
4. 그것이 제대로 작동되지 않아 유감입니다. 어쨌든, 다음 번에 더 잘 되기를 바랍니다.
5. 당신은 설명은 이치에 맞지만, 나는 여전히 그 계획이 실행 될 거라고 생각하지 않습니다.

Task 17

Answers:

1. Rug
2. Sofa and cushions
3. Window
4. Curtains
5. Picture
6. Lamp
7. Coffee table
8. Futon with a book and game

Translation:

1. 카펫
2. 소파와 쿠션
3. 창문

4. 커튼
5. 그림
6. 전등
7. 커피 테이블
8. 책과 게임기가 있는 소파 겸 침대

18 Task

Answers:

1. a 2. d 3. b

Translation:

1. 이 장면은 어디입니까?
   a. 바닷가
   b. 공원
   c. 누군가의 집에 있는 정원
   d. 수영장

2. 아래의 설명 중 위의 장면 속 사람들을 묘사하지 않는 것은 무엇입니까?
   a. 산책하고 있는 가족
   b. 일광욕을 하고 있는 사람들
   c. 파도에서 놀고 있는 아이
   d. 병원에 있는 개

3. 아래 중 어느 것이 이 장면을 가장 잘 묘사하고 있습니까?
   a. 해는 바다 너머로 지고 있습니다. 모래사장에는 많은 동물들이 있습니다.
   b. 일요일마다 바닷가는 사람들로 붐빕니다. 많은 가족들이 일광욕을 하고 있고, 파라솔 아래에서 그늘을 즐깁니다. 어린이들과 어른들은 수영을 하고 해변에서 즐겁게 뛰놉니다. 모두들 바닷가에서 하루를 보내는 것을 좋아합니다.
   c. 공원에서 자전거를 타고 있는 남자가 있습니다. 가족들도 있고, 조깅을 하는 사람들도 있습니다. 또한 한 커플이 벤치에 앉아 있습니다. 공원이 있습니다.
   d. 보기 중에 답이 없음.

Task 19

Answers:

I will never forget the classroom **of** my first school. **At** the front was a huge blackboard, and **at** the back was a big playing area. Our teacher always brought fresh flowers **to** the classroom and put them **next to** her desk. **Inside** her desk she kept lots of candy, and **under** the desk a big pair of fuzzy slippers. Desks were arranged **across** the room, and **between** the desks animal prints were painted **in** various colors **on** the floor. We always felt safe and happy **in** that room.

Translation:

나는 내 첫 번째 학교의 교실을 절대 잊을 수 없을 것입니다. 앞쪽에는 큰 칠판이 있었고, 뒤편에는 놀 수 있는 큰 공간이 있었습니다. 우리 선생님은 항상 교실에 신선한 꽃들을 가져왔고 그녀의 책상 옆에 그것들을 두었습니다. 그녀는 책상 안에 많은 사탕을 두었고, 책상 아래에는 보풀이 있는 슬리퍼 한 켤레가 있었습니다. 책상들은 교실을 가로질러 배열되어 있었습니다. 책상 사이사이 바닥에는 동물무늬가 다양한 색으로 칠해져 있었습니다. 우리는 항상 그 교실에서 마음이 놓였고 행복했습니다.

Task 20

Answers:

1. In the center of the field
2. from the waterfall, onto the rocks beneath.
3. Under the stars
4. Near the entrance
5. After dinner, in the house

Translation:

1. 경기장 중앙에 마운드가 있습니다.
2. 폭포로부터 물이 아래에 있는 바위에 튀깁니다.
3. 별들 아래, 쳐다보는 사람들과 춤추고 있는 아이들이 있습니다.
4. 입구 근처에 높은 문이 있는 울타리가 있습니다.
5. 저녁 식사 후에 집안은 조용해 집니다.

Task 21

Answers:

1. In Hawaii, there is a great place to spend a getaway weekend.
2. Around each villa, there is a beautiful garden.
3. Upon your arrival, the hotel staff brings you to your villa.
4. Outside near the beach is a small private pool.
5. Outside the patio there is also a spacious balcony.

Translation:

1. 하와이에는 주말 휴가를 보낼 수 있는 좋은 장소가 있습니다.
2. 각각의 빌라 주변에는 아름다운 정원이 있습니다.
3. 당신이 도착하자 마자, 호텔 직원이 당신을 빌라로 데려다 줍니다.
4. 해변 근처 밖에는 작은 개인 수영장이 있습니다.
5. 테라스 밖에는 넓은 발코니가 있습니다.

Task 22

Answers:

1. b 2. a 3. d 4. e 5. c

Translation:

1. 날이 너무 추워서 손가락에 감각이 없었습니다.
2. 표지판이 너무 작아서 바로 그 앞을 지나쳐서 운전했습니다.
3. 수업이 너무 지루해서 모두 잠이 들었습니다.
4. 그의 눈빛이 너무 강렬해서 나는 그를 쳐다볼 수가 없었습니다.
5. 너무나 당혹스러운 상황이어서 나는 그 상황과 관련된 모든 것을 잊고 싶습니다.

Task 23

Sample answers:

1A: The characters' names in *The Brothers Karamazov* are so difficult that I can neverremember them.

1B: *The Brothers Karamazov* is such a challenging book that it takes some people several years to finish it.

2A: New York is so far away that I seldom get the chance to visit.

2B: New York has such a lovely night skyline that you'll never forget it.

Translation:

예: 나의 여동생은 정말 열심히 공부해서 밥을 먹을 시간도 없습니다.
나의 여동생은 정말 훌륭한 학생이어서 시험을 망친 적이 한번도 없습니다.

1A: 카라마조프가의 형제들에 나오는 등장인물들의 이름은 너무 어려워서 나는 절대 그것을 기억할 수가 없습니다.

1B: 카라마조프가의 형제들은 정말 어려운 책이라서 어떤 사람들에게는 그것을 다 읽는데 몇 년이 걸리기도 합니다.

2A: 뉴욕은 정말 멀어서 나는 방문할 기회를 거의 갖지 못합니다.

2B: 뉴욕은 정말 아름다운 야경을 가지고 있어서 당신은 절대 그것을 잊지 못할 것입니다.

Unit 8

Comprehension questions

Answers:

1. (4)　　2. (2)　　3. (2)

Translation:

1. Fred는 왜 그의 상사를 위해서 선물을 샀습니까?
   (1) 그녀의 도움이 감사를 표하기 위해
   (2) 그녀로부터 더 나은 대우를 받기 위해
   (3) 실수에 대해 사과하기 위해
   (4) 우호적으로 대하기 위해서

2. 다음 중 상사의 행동에 대해서 Katherine이 설명한 내용이 아닌 것은?
   (1) 상사는 예의를 지켰다.
   (2) 상사는 그 선물을 좋아하지 않았다.
   (3) 상사는 다르게 대해야 한다는 부담을 느꼈다.
   (4) 상사는 과중한 부담감을 느꼈다.

3. Katherine은 왜 민호가 Fred에게 커피를 가져다 주었다고 생각하나요?
   (1) Fred가 수업 중에 집중할 수 있도록 돕기 위해
   (2) 그의 지각을 보상하기 위해
   (3) 그가 다시는 늦지 않을 것이란 다짐을 보이기 위해
   (4) 친절하게 대하기 위해서

Task 1

Answers:

1. First of all　　2. Second

3. Also　　　　　　　　4. Third
5. In addition

Translation:

개들이 최고의 애완동물이라는 것에는 세 가지 이유가 있습니다. 우선 첫 번째, 개들은 충성심이 매우 높습니다. 일단 개가 당신을 신뢰하면, 그는 항상 당신의 동반자가 되어줄 것입니다. 두 번째, 그들은 재미있습니다. 당신은 개를 산책시킬 수 있고, 던진 것 물어오기 놀이를 할 수도 있고, 심지어 수영도 함께 할 수 있습니다. 또한, 개들은 당신의 어린 아이들과 놀아주기 때문에 전체 가족에게 즐거움을 주게 됩니다. 세 번째, 개들은 위험에서 매우 잘 지켜줍니다. 당신이 강도에 관해 걱정을 한다면, 개는 모든 이에게 알리기 위해 크게 짖을 것이 분명합니다. 게다가, 개들은 일상 생활에서 장님들을 보호 해줄 수 있습니다.

Task 2

Answers:

1. First / First of all
2. Second
3. also
4. In addition / Finally

Translation:

몇 가지 종류의 지능이 있습니다. 첫 번째, 수학-논리 지능이 있습니다. 이 지능을 많이 가진 사람들은 보통 수학자, 기술자 또는 과학자가 됩니다. 두 번째, 언어 지능이 있습니다. 높은 언어 지능을 지닌 사람들은 언어 활용능력이 뛰어나기 때문에, 작가나 시인이 됩니다. 우리는 이 두 가지 지능에 친숙합니다. 또한 공간과 음악 지능이 있습니다. 음악 지능은 음악가, 가수들과 작곡가들에게 당연히 필요한 반면, 공간 지능은 예술가, 도시 계획가, 그리고 건축가들에게 필요합니다. 게다가 신체-운동 지능이 있는데, 댄서들, 운동선수들, 경찰관들 그리고 소방수들은 높은 신체-운동 지능을 가지고 있습니다. 마지막 두 개는 대인관계와 개인 내의 지능 입니다. 이런 종류의 지능은 대부분 지도자, 관리자, 그리고 주최자들에게서 발견됩니다. 결론적으로, "똑똑함"에는 여러 가지 면이 있습니다.

Task 3

Sample answer:

There are so many different types of food that I love, so I will just mention my top three. First, I absolutely adore Thai food. It has the perfect combination of heat, freshness, and complex flavor. I eat it as often as I can. Second, I am a huge fan of Mexican food. Like Thai food, it is quite spicy, but it usually leaves a heavier feeling in my stomach because of its liberal use of fatty ingredients like cheese and sour cream. Third, I can't go a week without having Korean food. Even though it uses only four main spices, there is something very addictive about the kimchi and spicy fermented bean paste that are part of most Korean meals.

Translation:

제가 좋아하는 음식의 종류는 정말 많습니다. 그렇기 때문에 제가 가장 좋아하는 음식을 세 가지만 꼽아보도록 하겠습니다. 첫째, 저는 정말로 태국음식을 좋아합니다. 태국음식은 열, 신선함, 그리고 다채로운 향이 완벽하게 조화되어 있습니다. 저는 태국음식을 자주 먹을 수 있는 만큼 먹습니다. 둘째, 저는 멕시코 음식의 진정한 팬입니다. 태국음식과 마찬가지로, 멕시코음식은 꽤 맵습니다. 그러나 멕시코 음식은 태국음식에 비해 뱃속에 조금 더 묵직한 느낌을 남기는데, 이것은 치즈나 사어크림과 같은 지방성 재료들을 자유로이 사용하기 때문입니다. 셋째, 저는 한국음식이 없이는 일주일도 버티지 못합니다. 네 개의 주 양념들만 사용했을 뿐이지만, 대부분의 한국 식사에서 찾아볼 수 있는 김치와 고추장에는 묘한 중독성이 있습니다.

Task 4

Answers:

My husband and I get along <u>well</u>, but our personalities are <u>completely</u> different. He talks, walks, eats and drinks <u>very</u> <u>slowly</u>, but I do everything quickly. He wakes up early every day, but I love to sleep late. He is quite passionate about his job and works diligently, but I hate my job and do it unenthusiastically. His side of the bedroom is neat and tidy, but my half is so messy. He drives slowly and cautiously, but I don't have the patience for that, so he thinks I am a dangerous driver. But I think these things are not really important. We love each other deeply and never fight at all, so I think we will live happily ever after.

Translation:

남편과 나는 잘 지내지만 우리의 성격은 완전히 다릅니다. 그는 매우 천천히 말하고, 걷고, 먹고, 그리고 마시지만 나는 모든 것을 빠르게 합니다. 그는 매일 일찍 일어나지만, 나는 늦게까지 자는 것을 좋아합니다. 그는 그의 직업에 관해 꽤 열정적이고 열심히 일을 하지만 나는 나의 직업을 싫어하고 열성 없이 일을 합니다. 그의 쪽 침실은 깔끔하고 정리정돈되어 있지만 내 쪽은 매우 지저분합니다. 그는 천천히 그리고 조심스럽게 운전을 하지만 나는 운전 할 때 참을성이 없어서 그는 나를 위험한 운전자라고 생각합니다. 그러나 나는 이런 것들이 별로 중요하다고 생각하지 않습니다. 우리는 서로를 깊게 사랑하고 싸우는 일이 없어서 우리는 행복하게 오래오래 살 것이라고 생각합니다.

Task 5

Answers:

1. reckless/ recklessly
2. impatiently/ impatient
3. angry/angrily
4. happily/happy
5. noisy/noisily

Translation:

1. 나의 오빠는 무모한 운전자 입니다. 그는 항상 무모하게 운전을 하며 우리가 아무리 천천히 운전하도록 설득을 하려 노력해도 소용이 없습니다.
2. 배고픈 여행자들은 가이드가 그 빌딩에 대한 긴 역사를 설명해주는 동안 조급한 마음으로 들었습니다. 여행 그룹의 한 일원은 너무 조급해져서 식당으로 간식을 먹으러

갔습니다.

3. 화가 난 시위자들이 대 광장을 향해서 행진 했습니다. 그리고 나서, 경찰들이 바리케이드를 설치하려고 시작하자, 군중들은 경찰들에게 분노하여서 소리쳤습니다.
4. 나는 나의 잃어버린 개를 찾아주는 사람에게 기쁘게 보상을 지급할 것입니다. 그녀는 검은 털을 가진 크고 멋진 래브라도 리트리버 입니다.
5. 지난 주에 길 아래 식당에서 시끄러운 파티가 있었습니다. 사람들이 밤새 시끄럽게 얘기하고 노래한 탓에 나는 잠을 잘 수 없었습니다.

Unit 9

Task 1

Answers:

(1) hope to have
(2) a harmonious family
(3) a thoughtful man
(4) hobbies and interests similar to mine; the same hobbies and interests as me; the same hobbies and interests that I do/have

Translation:

이상적인 남편

나는 미래에 헌신적인 남편과 화목한 가족을 갖기를 원합니다. 그렇기 때문에, 나의 이상적인 남편은 건전한 사고방식을 갖춘 사려 깊은 남자입니다. 또한, 집안일에 대해 긍정적인 태도를 가지고, 육아와 가사일을 도와주어야 합니다. 나아가, 그는 나와 같은 취미와 흥미를 가져야 합니다. 이것이 내가 생각하는 완벽한 남편이지만, 정말 이런 사람을 찾을 수 있을까요?

Task 2

Answers:

1. b 2. a 3. b 4. a 5. a

Translation:

1. 다음 중 주제 문장의 예로 가장 적합한 것은 무엇인가요?
   a. 여름에, 당신은 수영을 할 수 있습니다.
   b. 해변은 여름에도 겨울에도 즐겁습니다.
   c. 또한, 맑은 겨울 밤에, 모닥불 주위에 앉는 것은 즐겁습니다.
   d. 수영을 하고 싶지 않다면, 모래 위에 앉아서 쉬어도 좋습니다.

2. 다음 문장을 읽어보세요:
   훌륭한 건축가는 예술가이자 수학자입니다.

   주제가 무엇입니까?
   a. 훌륭한 건축가
   b. 예술가와 수학자

3. 다음 문장을 읽어보세요:
   예술적 재능과 수학적 능력은 훌륭한 건축가의 2가지 자질입니다.

   생각을 밝히는 부분은 무엇입니까?
   a. 훌륭한 건축가
   b. 예술적 재능과 수학적 능력

4. 주제 문장은 독자가 무엇을 읽을지 알려줍니다.
   a. 참
   b. 거짓

5. 생각 밝히기 부분은 독자에게 단락에서 무슨 주제에 대해 논의할지를 알려줍니다.
   a. 참
   b. 거짓

Task 3

Answers:

1. Of course, sometimes they cannot go out because of their health.
2. My sister also has a dog named Gregory.

Translation:

1.

노년층

많은 노년층이 직면하는 또 다른 문제점은 줄어든 수입으로 사는 것입니다. 은퇴를 하면, 노년층은 그들의 회사로부터 연금을 받거나 정부로부터 복지혜택을 받습니다. 노인들의 한 달 수입은 그들이 고용되었을 때와 비교하면 현저하게 적습니다. 갑자기 은퇴자들은 더 이상 익숙해진 삶의 방식대로 살아갈 수 없다는 것을 알게 됩니다. 그 삶의 방식이 검소했을지라도 말이죠. 많은 사람들은, 그들의 월 고지서를 낸 후에, 영화나 외식을 위해 쓸 돈이 남아있지 않다는 것을 알게 됩니다. 물론, 때로는 그들의 건강 때문에 밖에 못나가기도 합니다. 일부 노년층은, 그들이 받는 적은 돈으로 월 고지서들을 감당하지 못하기도 합니다. 그들은 전기, 전화 그리고 좋은 음식들이 사치품이며 그들이 더 이상 그것들을 살 능력이 안 된다는 사실을 공포와 함께 깨닫습니다.

2.

Gregory

by Barbara Carter

그레고리는 내 아름다운 회색 페르시안 고양이입니다. 그는 도도하고 우아하게, 섬세한 발레댄서처럼 느릿하게 각 발을 올리고 내리면서 무시의 춤사위를 펼치듯이 걷습니다. 그러나 겉모습에서는 그러한 도도함을 찾아볼 수 없는데, 대부분의 시간 동안 집안에서 텔레비전을 봐서 살이 쪘기 때문입니다. 고양이 사료 광고와의 친숙함은 그레고리로 하여금 일반 브랜드의 사료를 거부하고 가장 비싼 브랜드의 사료만을 고집하게 만들었습니다. 그레고리는 먹이를 대할 때와 마찬가지로 방문객들에게도 까다롭습니다. 일부 사람들에게는 친근하게 대하고 일부 사람들은 내쫓습니다. 그는 당신의 발목에 기대며 바싹 달라붙어서, 쓰다듬어 달라고 애원하거나, 스컹크를 흉내 내며 당신이 좋아하는 바지를 더럽힐 수도 있습니다. 많은 고양이 전문가들이 생각하듯이 그레고리가 자신의 영역을 나타내기 위해 이렇게 행동하는 것은 아닙니다. 제 친구들을 질투하기 때문에 제 기분을 상하게 만들기 위해 그렇게 행동하는 것입니다. 제 여동생도 그레고리라는 이름을 가진 개를 가지고 있습니다. 제 손님들이 떠난 후에, 저는 텔레비전 앞에서 혼자 미소를 지으면서 졸고 있는 늙은 고양이를 쳐다봤습니다. 그리고 괘씸하지만 애정이 담긴 습관을 지닌 그레고리를 용서해야만 했습니다.

Task 4

Answers:

1. b
2. Though this experience was upsetting, and a huge culture shock, it will stay with me forever.

Translation:

1. 역사를 통해서 볼 때 사람들은 지렁이가 중요하다는 것을 이해하고 있습니다.
2. 비록 이 경험은 즐겁지 않고, 큰 문화 충격이었지만, 제 안에 평생 남을 것입니다.

모든 역사를 통해서 사람들은 지렁이가 지구의 옥토를 기름지게 하는데 필수적이라는 것을 알고 있었습니다. 이집트 여왕 클레오파트라는 지렁이를 신성하다고 여겼습니다. 그리스 철학자 아리스토텔레스는 지렁이가 토양의 장이라고 말했습니다. 1881년 찰스 다윈은 "세계 역사에서 그렇게 중요한 역할을 한 다른 창조물인 많이 있는 것 같지 않다" 라고 말했습니다.

Task 5

Sample answers:

1. Some people like cats and some people like dogs, but I like turtles.
2. Kittens are soft, fuzzy and cute. They like to play and take naps.

3. Puppies are cute, too, but they can't protect you.
4. Dogs are loyal friends. They comfort you, welcome you home after work, and protect you.
5. Lions and tigers are good protectors, but they eat too much food.
6. Monkeys like to swing around and play, but they are a little stinky.
7. Turtles are peaceful, gentle and wise, so they are the best pets.

Translation:

1. 몇몇 사람들은 고양이를 좋아하고 몇몇 사람들은 개를 좋아하지만, 나는 거북이를 좋아합니다.
2. 새끼 고양이들은 부드럽고, 복슬복슬하고 그리고 귀엽습니다. 그들은 놀기와 낮잠자기를 좋아합니다.
3. 강아지들 또한 귀엽지만, 그들은 당신을 보호할 수 없습니다.
4. 개들은 충성스러운 친구들입니다. 그들은 당신을 편안하게 해주고, 퇴근한 후에 당신을 반갑게 맞아주며 그리고 당신을 보호해줍니다.
5. 사자와 호랑이는 훌륭한 보호자이지만 그들은 음식을 너무 많이 먹습니다.
6. 원숭이들은 여기저기 매달려 다니고 노는 것을 좋아하지만, 그들은 조금 냄새가 납니다.
7. 거북이들은 평화롭고, 부드럽고 그리고 현명하기 때문에, 최고의 애완동물입니다.

Task 6

Answers:

Although many people think that women are weaker than men, they are actually superior to men in many ways. In most countries, women live longer and are healthier than men. Women are better than men at doing things that involve the five senses. For example, they have a stronger sense of smell and of taste. What's more, they have better vision and hearing. Although women are on average physically weaker than men, they are mentally stronger. Men are more violent than women and commit more crimes, but women are more compassionate and forgiving. If you consider all of these points, you cannot deny that women are better than men.

Translation:

1. 많은 사람들은 여성이 남성보다 약하다고 생각하지만, 여성들은 실로 남성들보다 많은 면에서 우수합니다.
2. 대부분의 나라들에서 여자들은 남자들보다 더 오래 살며, 그들은 남자들보다 더 건강하게 삽니다.
3. 여자들은 오감을 포함하는 이런 것들을 할 때 남자들보다 더 잘합니다.
4. 여자들은 더 발달된 후각을 가지고 있고, 그들은 더 발달된 미각을 가지고 있고 그들은 더 발달된 시각과 청각을 가지고 있습니다.
5. 평균적인 여성들은 남성들보다 신체적으로는 약하지만, 정신적으로는 남성들보다 더 강합니다.
6. 남성들은 여성들보다 더 폭력적이고 그들은 더 많은 범죄를 저지릅니다. 여성들은 동정심과 관대한 마음을 가지고 있습니다.
7. 이러한 점들을 고려해보면 여성이 더 우월하다는 것을 부인할 수 없습니다.

비록 많은 사람들이 여성들이 남성보다 약하다고 생각하지만, 여성들은 실제로 많은 면에 있어 남성보다 우월합니다. 대부분의 나라에서, 여성들은 남성들보다 더 오래 그리고 더 건강하게 삽니다. 여성들은 오감을 포함하는 것들을 할 때 남성들 보다 더 잘합니다. 예를 들면, 그들은 더 발달된 후각과 미각을 가지고 있습니다. 게다가, 그들은 더 발달된 시각과 청각을 가지고 있습니다. 비록 여성들이 평균적으로 남성들보다 신체적으로 약하지만, 정신적으로는 더 강합니다. 남성들은 여성들보다 더 폭력적이고 더 많은 범죄를 저지르지만, 여성들은 더 많은 동정심과 관대한 마음을 가지고 있습니다. 만약 당신이 이 모든 점들을 고려한다면, 여성이 남성보다 우월하다는 것을 부인할 수 없습니다.

Unit 10

Comprehension questions

Answers:

1. (1) 2. (4) 3. (2) 4. (3) 5. (4)

Translation:

1. 다음 단어 중 Katherine이 라운지에 들어섰을 때의 기분을 가장 잘 표현한 것은?
   (1) 흥분된
   (2) 화난
   (3) 후회하는
   (4) 호기심이 많은

2. Katherine은 주로 그녀의 부모님과 어떻게 연락을 하나요?
   (1) 이메일로
   (2) 전화로
   (3) 문자메시지를 통해서
   (4) Skype를 이용해서

3. Fred는 왜 Skype를 사용하지 않나요?
   (1) 그는 시간이 없다.
   (2) 그는 그것을 사용하는 것이 겁난다.
   (3) 너무 비싸다.
   (4) 너무 편리하다.

4. Katherine은 왜 Fred를 '할아버지' 라고 부르나요?
   (1) 그는 그녀보다 훨씬 나이가 많다.
   (2) 그는 덥수룩한 턱수염을 가지고 있다.
   (3) 그는 구식이다.
   (4) 그는 실제로 그녀의 할아버지이다.

5. Fred가 "진짜" 편지를 좋아하는 이유가 아닌 것은?
   (1) 그가 실제로 편지를 만질 수 있기 때문에
   (2) 그가 냄새를 맡을 수 있기 때문에
   (3) 글 쓴 사람의 영혼을 좀 더 가까이 느낄 수 있기 때문에
   (4) 쓰는데 시간이 걸리기 때문에

Task 1

Sample answers:

Northern California (Title)

Topic Sentence: Northern California is a fantastic place to go on a vacation for two reasons.

Reason A: First of all, Northern California has an amazing amount of state parks, as well as national parks where one can see spectacular flora and fauna.

Example 1: In Redwood State Park, for example, tourists are able to see Sequoia trees as old as fifteen-hundred years.

Example 2: On the coast, at JV Fitzgerald Marine Reserve, travelers can observe seals nesting, mating, and giving birth.

Reason B: Secondly, Northern California has some of the greatest mountains for hiking and climbing in the world.

Example 1: Take Mount Shasta for example, in Shasta-Trinity National Forest.

Example 2: The Sierra Nevada Mountains in Yosemite Park are accessible by car and are breathtaking.

Concluding Sentence: Indeed, Northern California is a wonderful place to go if you like the wilderness.

Translation:

북부 캘리포니아 (주제)

주제 문장: 북부 캘리포니아는 두 가지 이유에서 휴가 때 방문하기에 환상적인 곳입니다.

근거 A: 우선 첫 번째로, 북부 캘리포니아는 다양한 동식물들을 볼 수 있는 국립공원들 뿐만 아니라, 놀랄 만큼 많은 수의 주립공원들을 가지고 있습니다.

예시1: 예를 들어, Redwood 주립공원에서, 방문객들은 1500년 가량 된 Sequoia 나무들을 볼 수 있습니다.

예시 2: 해변가의, JV Firzgerald 해양보호 구역에서, 여행자들은 물개들이 둥지를 틀고, 짝짓기를 하고, 출산하는 모습을 관찰할 수 있습니다.

근거 B: 둘째로, 북부 캘리포니아는 하이킹과 등산을 하기에 좋은 세계적으로 훌륭한 산들이 있습니다.

예시 1: Shasta-Trinity 국립 숲에 있는 Shasta산을 예로 들어 봅시다.
예시 2: Yosemite 공원에 있는 Sierra Nevada 산은 자동차로 접근할 수 있고 숨이 막힐 정도로 아름답습니다.
결론 문장: 당신이 야생을 좋아한다면 북부 캘리포니아는 가 보아야 할 정말 멋진 곳입니다.

Task 2

Sample answers:

Small cars are more economical than big cars. (Topic)
A. They don't use much gasoline (Reason)
  1. A Honda Civic gets forty miles per gallon. (Example)
  2. Small cars are lighter and have more efficient engines than big cars. (Example)
B. Maintenance costs are lower. (Reason)
  1. Since cars are smaller, the parts are cheaper to fix. (Example)
  2. Small cars cost less to have cleaned than large cars. (Example)
C. Insurance is cheaper. (Reason)
  1. Smaller cars are cheaper to fix; Thus insurance is cheaper. (Example)
  2. Smaller cars can't cause much damage in accidents. (Example)
You save money on gas, maintenance and insurance when you own a small car.

Translation:

소형차들이 대형차들에 비해 경제적입니다. (주제)
A. 휘발유를 많이 사용하지 않습니다. (이유)
  1. 혼다 시빅은 1갤론에 40마일을 달릴 수 있습니다. (예시)
  2. 작은 차는 큰 차보다 더 가볍고 더 효율적인 엔진을 가지고 있습니다. (예시)
B. 차량 유지비가 적게 듭니다. (이유)
  1. 차가 작기 때문에, 수리하기 위한 부품비가 더 저렴합니다. (예시)
  2. 작은 차는 큰 차보다 세차비가 적게 듭니다. (예시)

C. 보험료가 더 저렴합니다. (이유)

1. 소형차들은 수리비가 더 저렴하기 때문에, 보험료가 더 저렴합니다. (예시)
2. 사고가 났을 때 큰 손상을 초래하지 않습니다. (예시)

소형차를 소유하면 기름, 유지비, 그리고 보험료에 들어가는 돈을 절약할 수 있습니다.

Task 3

Sample answers:

CUFS (Title)

Topic Sentence: I chose to attend CUFS for two reasons: flexibility and interaction.

Reason A: First, CUFS is an online university.

Example 1: Unlike traditional schools, CUFS allows students the flexibility to attend lectures and do work online.

Example 2: Since I'm a stay-at-home mom, an online program allows me to work at my own pace from the comfort of my own.

Reason B: Second, there are many opportunities to interact and engage with others.

Example 1: Although most courses are online, they also offer special real-time interactive video sessions every week, as well as offline classes on Saturdays.

Example 2: In addition, there are opportunities to meet other students through the internet and when we have time, we can meet in person.

Concluding Sentence: Even though it is an online university, CUFS offers an education with more flexibility and access to professors and other students on my own terms.

Translation:

CUFS (주제)

주제 문장: 저는 융통성과 상호작용이라는 두 가지 이유에서 CUFS를 선택했습니다.

이유 A: 첫 번째로, CUFS는 온라인 대학입니다.

예시 1: 전통적인 학교와는 달리, CUFS는 강의수강과 숙제를 온라인으로 할 수 있는 융통성을 학생에게 허용합니다.

예시 2: 전업주부인 저에게, 온라인 프로그램은 저의 페이스에 맞추어 집에서 편안히 공부하는 것을 허용합니다.

이유 B: 두 번째로, 다른 사람들과 상호작용하고 관계를 맺을 수 있는 기회를 많이 제공합니다.

예시 1: 대부분의 수업들이 온라인이지만, 토요일 오프라인 수업뿐만 아니라 실시간 비디오 세션을 제공합니다.

예시 2: 게다가 인터넷을 통해 다른 학생들을 만날 기회가 있고, 시간이 생길 때면 실제로 만날 수도 있습니다.

결론 문장: 온라인에 기반을 둔 대학이긴 하지만, CUFS는 보다 융통성 있는 교육을 제공하고 교수님들 그리고 다른 학생들과 제가 원할 때 접촉을 할 수 있도록 해줍니다.

Task 4

Sample answers:

(1) The second reason is that the food is fresh and delicious.

(2) Second, it can help you to expand your understanding of the world.

(3) The second is its dedicated team of support staff.

Translation:

1. 제주도는 한국에서 여행하기 좋은 곳입니다.
   첫 번째 이유는 날씨가 항상 좋기 때문입니다. 두 번째 이유는 음식이 신선하고 맛있게 때문입니다.
2. 해외에서 공부하는 것에는 좋은 이유들이 많이 있습니다.
   우선 첫 번째로, 외국어 실력을 향상 시키기에 좋은 기회입니다. 두 번째로, 세상에 대한 이해를 넓히는데 도움을 줄 수 있습니다.
3. CUFS가 다른 온라인 대학들에 비해 우수한 데는 몇 가지 이유들이 있습니다.
   첫 번째는 양질의 교육을 위한 교원들의 노력입니다. 두 번째는 CUFS의 헌신적인 지원 팀입니다.

Task 5

Answers:

1. For example, / For instance,
2. For example, / For instance,
3. such as / like / including
4. such as / like
5. For example, / For instance,
6. such as / like

Translation:

1. 홍콩에는 다양한 건축양식들이 있습니다. 예를 들어, 섬의 끝 쪽으로 가면 당신은 오래된 절과 다른 전통적인 건물들을 볼 수 있을 것입니다.
2. 현대적인 건축물들의 좋은 예시들도 많이 있습니다. 예를 들어, 중심적인 상업지구에서 당신은 몇몇의 독특하고 영감을 주는 초고층건물들을 볼 수 있습니다.
3. 음식 또한 도시로 사람들을 유인하는 주요 요인입니다. 한국에서 파는 중국음식을 즐기는 사람들을 위해서, 만두와 국수와 같은 인기 있는 음식은 거의 모든 곳에서 찾아 볼 수 있습니다.
4. 당신이 만약 모험을 해보고 싶다면, "사천샤부샤부"와 "화추연"와 같은 맵고 톡 쏘는 요리를 먹기 위해 "조조의 복수"로 가세요.
5. 만약 어린이가 있다면, 갈 수 있는 많은 인기명소들이 있습니다. 예를 들어 / 예를 들자면, 오션파크는 당신의 아이들이 하루 종일 즐거운 상태로 있을 수 있게 해줍니다.
6. 마지막으로, 당신은 관광으로 긴 하루를 보낸 후 호텔로 돌아가 실내 온천풀, VIP 마사지룸 그리고 우리의 유명한 "금성" 노래방과 같은 시설들을 즐길 수 있습니다.

Unit 11

Task 1

Sample answers:

(1) To my dear sister,; Dear sister,

(2) struggling with your daily routine

(3) my wife is pregnant; my wife has become pregnant; my wife is expecting

(4) how to be

Translation:

사랑하는 나의 누나에게

10월의 첫째 날입니다. 누난 매일매일의 일과와 고군분투하며 조카 혜윤이와 집에 있겠군요. 내가 조카를 놀보는데 도움을 줄 수 있으면 좋으련만, 나는 지금 나의 상황 때문에 그럴 수 있는 여유가 없습니다. 나는 일 때문에 너무 바쁩니다. 그리고 누나도 알다시피, 내 부인이 임신을 했습니다. 누나가 한 아이의 부모이기에 나는 정말 누나를 존경하고 누나가 좋은 부모가 되는 법을 알려줘서 너무나 감사합니다. 누나의 두 번째 임신 소식을 들으니 정말 놀랍습니다. 축하해요 누나! 나는 우리의 새 아기들이 서로에게 좋은 사촌이 될 거라고 확신합니다. 나는 항상 누나의 편에서 있으니, 내가 필요할 때는 언제든 말하세요.

사랑을 담아,

기석

Task 2

Answers:

1. IC　　2. DC　　3. IC　　4. IC　　5. DC

Translation:

1. 블록 주변에서 산책을 합니다.
2. 내가 일하러 가기 전에
3. 요가는 내 몸을 깨워주고 마음을 정리해 줍니다.
4. 겨울에 이것을 하는 건 어렵습니다.
5. 내가 일하러 갈 때 여전히 어둡기 때문에

Task 3

Answers:

1. before
2. after
3. while
4. Although
5. if

Translation:

1. 당신이 길을 건너기 전에 초록 불이 될 때까지 기다리세요.
2. 이 운동을 끝내고 난 후에 나는 바로 자러 갈 것입니다.
3. 내가 자려고 하는 동안, 나의 이웃들은 파티를 열고 있었습니다.
4. 나의 아버지는 비록 오랫동안 플로리다에 사셨지만, 영어를 하지 못하십니다.
5. 만약 나의 남자친구가 밸런타인데이에 나에게 꽃을 사 준다면, 나는 행복할 것입니다.

Task 4

Sample answers:

1. I always eat breakfast before I go to school.
2. I try to finish all my work at the office because it is late when I get home.
3. Although I try to get up early even on weekends, I'm usually late to church
4. I become moody and depressed if I stay in the house all day.
5. I become cranky if I skip a meal.

Translation:

1. 학교 가기 전에 나는 항상 아침식사를 합니다.
2. 내가 집에 도착할 때는 늦기 때문에 나는 사무실에서 내 일을 끝내려 노력합니다.
3. 나는 주말에도 일찍 일어나려 노력하지만, 보통 교회에 늦습니다.
4. 하루 종일 집에 미무른다면, 나는 서글퍼 지고 우울해 집니다.
5. 식사를 거르면, 나는 짜증을 냅니다.

Task 5

Answers:

1. (complex), Many people like to stay at home when they have time off.
2. (compound), Some people like to visit relatives, and others like to travel abroad.
3. (simple), Lately "extreme" vacations are becoming more and more popular.
4. (simple), For instance, some extreme vacationers go alligator hunting in Australia or bungee jumping in New Zealand.
5. (compound), Some people enjoy spending their holiday indoors with a good book, while others spend their free time doing volunteer work.

6. (complex), Opportunities for volunteer work are increasing because so many people in the world need help.
7. (compound), Students often want to make the most of their time, so they spend their vacations cramming for examinations.

Translation:

1. (복문), 일이 없을 때에 많은 사람들은 집에 있는 것을 좋아합니다.
2. (중문), 어떤 사람들은 친척집을 방문하는 것을 좋아합니다. 그리고 다른 사람들은 해외여행 하는 것을 좋아합니다.
3. (단문), 최근에 "익스트림" 휴가가 점점 더 인기를 얻고 있습니다.
4. (단문), 예를 들어, 익스트림 휴가를 보내는 사람들은 호주로 악어사냥을 가기도 하고, 뉴질랜드로 번지점프를 하러 가기도 합니다.
5. (중문), 어떤 사람들은 휴일을 좋은 책과 함께 실내에서 보내는 것을 좋아하지만, 반면 다른 사람들은 자원봉사 활동을 하면서 자유시간을 보내기도 합니다.
6. (복문), 세상에 정말 많은 사람들이 도움을 필요로 하기 때문에 자원봉사 활동에 대한 기회가 늘고 있습니다.
7. (중문) 학생들은 시간을 최대한 활용하고자 합니다. 그래서 학생들은 그들의 휴가를 시험을 위한 벼락치기 공부를 하는데 씁니다.

Task 6

Answers:

1. (F) → Because so many students missed the exam, it was rescheduled.
2. (F) → I do thirty minutes of exercise before I eat breakfast.
3. (S)
4. (F) → Her legs were sore because she was out all night dancing.
5. (F) → Since she works hard and never misses a class, all the teachers love her.
6. (F) → Whenever he gets sick he switches to light cigarettes.
7. (S)

Translation:

1. 너무 많은 학생들이 시험을 놓쳤기 때문에 그것은 다시 조정되었다.
2. 나는 아침식사 전에 30분씩 운동을 합니다.
3. 나는 우산 가지고 오는 것을 잊어서, 병이 들었습니다.
4. 그녀는 밖에서 밤새도록 춤을 췄기 때문에 다리가 아팠습니다.
5. 그녀는 성실하고 수업을 절대 빠지지 않기 때문에, 모든 선생님들이 그녀를 좋아합니다.
6. 그는 아플 때 마다 담배 태우기 위해 라이터를 켭니다.
7. 그는 시험이 있을 때만 늦게 오는 것처럼 보입니다.

Unit 12

Comprehension questions

Answers:

(1) 3 (2) 2 (3) 4 (4) 2 (5) 3

Translation:

1. Fred에 의하면 이 날 수업은 어땠나요?
   (1) 아주 훌륭했다.
   (2) 좋았다
   (3) 보통이었다
   (4) 끔찍했다.

2. 이 날 Fred의 학생을 가장 잘 묘사하는 단어는?
   (1) 흥분한
   (2) 피곤한
   (3) 우울한
   (4) 희망적인

3. 왜 Fred는 한국에서 아이를 기르고 싶을까요?
   (1) 한국 음식을 좋아해서
   (2) 한국교사들이 더 훌륭한 것 같아서
   (3) 한국의 학교가 가장 좋은 것 같아서
   (4) 한국학생들의 습관이 인상 깊어서

4. 한국교육에 대한 Katherine의 태도를 가장 잘 묘사한 단어는 무엇입니까?
   (1) 감동적이다.
   (2) 회의적이다
   (3) 긍정적이다
   (4) 무섭다

5. Katherine이 생각하는 미국학생들의 인상은 무엇입니까?
   (1) 일을 너무 많이 한다
   (2) 항상 운동을 한다
   (3) 취미가 다양하다
   (4) 미국학생들은 비디오게임을 너무 자주 한다.

Task 1

Answers:

(1) a (2) b (3) c (4) b (5) b

Translation:

나는 사형제도가 옳다고 생각하지 않습니다. 첫째, 나는 모든 살생은 잘못이라고 생각합니다. 인간들은 다른 사람의 삶을 박탈한 권리가 없습니다. 정부가 아닌, 오직 신만이 할 수 있습니다. 정부는 사람들로 만들어졌기 때문에 누군가를 죽여서는 안 됩니다. 설사 그 사람이 끔찍한 범죄를 저질렀다 할지라도 말입니다. 둘째, 사형 위협은 범죄를 예방하지 않습니다. 어떤 범죄자들도 잡힐 계획을 세우지는 않습니다. 그렇기 때문에 뒤따라 올 집행에 상관없이 범죄자들은 그들이 원하는 대로 행동할 것입니다. 사실, 주(州)의 사형 집행이 증가한

시기에 도시의 살인율은 심지어 증가하기도 합니다. 이와 같은 현상은 1987년 New Orleans에서 발생했습니다. 셋째, 그리고 가장 중요한 것은, 과학과 기술의 발전과 함께 이미 유죄 판결을 받은 범죄자의 무죄를 증명할 새로운 증거가 나타나는 것은 낯선 일이 아닙니다. 만약 이 같은 일이 이미 사형된 사람에게 발생한다면, 시간을 되돌릴 수 있는 방법이 없습니다. 이것이 현실이라기 보다는 헐리우드 이야기 같이 보이겠지만, 미국에서만 20명이 넘는 사람들이 20세기에 실수로 사형되었으며 이 수치는 확인된 사건들만 포함한 것입니다. 내 의견으로는, 이 경우들을 정부에 의한 살인 행위로 간주될 수 있습니다. 한마디로, 사형제도는 금지되어야 한다.

1. 글쓴이는 사형에 대해서 어떻게 생각합니까?
   a. 잘못된 것이다
   b. 옳은 것이다
   c. 옳은 것도 옳지 않은 것도 아니다
   d. 답 없음

2. 사형에 대한 글쓴이의 관점은 사실입니까 의견입니까?
   a. 사실
   b. 의견

3. 글쓴이는 몇 가지 이유를 썼습니까?
   a. 1
   b. 2
   c. 3
   d. 4

4. 이러한 이유들 중에 몇 가지가 사실입니까?
   a. 0
   b. 1
   c. 2
   d. 3

5. 글쓴이가 준 정보들은 전부 사실입니까 의견입니까?
   a. 전부 사실이다
   b. 몇 가지는 의견이다

Task 2

Answers:

1. In my view, no one should be allowed to own a gun.
2. I believe that riding a bicycle is the best mode of transportation.
3. I think cats are better pets than dogs.
4. In my opinion, everybody should go to school.
5. According to Mrs. Choi, her husband makes the best bibimbap.

Translation:

1. 내 관점으로는, 어느 누구도 총기소지가 허용되어서는 안 된다.
2. 나는 자전거가 가장 좋은 교통수단이라고 믿는다.
3. 나는 고양이들이 개보다 더 좋은 애완동물이라고 생각한다.
4. 내 의견으로는, 모든 사람들이 학교에 가야만 한다.
5. 최씨에 따르면, 그녀의 남편은 최고의 비빔밥을 만든다.

Task 3

Sample answers:

Topic: The minimum age for drinking in Korea.

Opinion: In my opinion, there should be no minimum age for drinking alcohol.

Support: In most countries, there is no minimum age. (fact)

Support: Parents, not the government, should decide if their children are mature enough to drink. (opinion)

Translation:

주제: 한국에서 음주할 수 있는 최소 연령

의견: 내 의견으로는, 음주에 대한 최소 연령은 없어져야 합니다.

뒷받침: 대부분의 나라에는 그러한 최소 연령은 없습니다. (사실)
뒷받침: 아이들이 술을 마실 만큼 성숙했는지는 정부가 아니라 부모가 결정해야 합니다.

Task 4

Answers:

1. which 2. who 3. who 4. which
5. who 6. which 7. who, which

Translation:

1. 많은 나라에서 여전히 보편적인 전통 결혼식에서는, 미래의 배우자가 다른 누군가에 의해 정해집니다.
2. 때때로 그들 자신보다 그들에 대해서 더 잘 알고 있는 엄마나 아빠가 결정을 합니다.
3. 다른 곳에서는 적절한 배우자를 찾아주는 결혼 중매인이 결정을 짓는다.
4. 부모님들과 만나는 첫 번째 만남이 어색한 것은 커플들에게 흔히 있는 일이다.
5. 중매결혼이 자유가 없다는 의미가 아니다. 남자든 여자든 정해진 배우자가 마음에 들지 않으면 다른 사람을 요구 할 수 있다.
6. 서양에서 흔히 있는 낭만적인 결혼식은 성공적이지 못한 것으로 드러난다.
7. 연애해서 결혼한 사람들이 중매로 결혼한 사람들보다 이혼할 확률이 더 높은데, 중매결혼이 더 안정적인 것처럼 보입니다.

Task 5

Answers:

1) which is located to the north of Busan
2) who dedicated her life to her family
3) who is deeply loved by all her students
4) which is the highest mountain in Korea

5) who was a great man
6) which is said to be "The Third City" of Korea

Translation:

1) 나의 고향은 부산 북쪽에 있는데, 아름다운 곳입니다.
2) 나는 엄마에게 항상 고마움을 느끼는데, 엄마는 일생 동안 가족을 위해서 헌신했습니다.
3) 모든 학생들로부터 사랑을 받는 성은경은 이 수업의 교수님이다.
4) 한라산은 한국에서 가장 높은 산인데, 제주도에 위치해 있습니다.
5) 훌륭한 사람이었던 노무현은 한국의 9번째 대통령이다.
6) IAFF 2011 World Championships는 한국의 세 번째 도시로 알려져 있는 대구에서 열린다.

Unit 13

Task 1

Answers:

(1) insist that (2) make sense (3) catch on
(4) confusing (5) depressed

Translation:

(1) 비록 당신이 몸이 좋지 않더라도, 나는 당신이 오늘 학교에 가야만 한다고 생각합니다.
(2) 우리 교수님은 정답이 C라고 말씀하셨지만, 나는 그 답이 이해가 되지 않습니다.
(3) 여기서 내가 그 시스템을 이해하는데 시간이 좀 걸렸지만, 나는 마침내 해낼 수 있었습니다.
(4) 11번 문제가 시험에서 가장 헷갈리는 문제였습니다.
(5) 그녀는 우울함을 느낄 때마다 낮잠을 잡니다.

Task 2

Answers:

1. First of all
2. Second
3. Also
4. Third
5. In addition

Translation:

고양이들은 세 가지 이유로 최고의 애완동물이라고 할 수 있습니다. 첫 번째로, 고양이들은 매우 독립적입니다. 먹이를 주고, 변기를 청소해주는 것을 제외하고는 고양이는 스스로 자신들을 돌보기 때문에 당신은 한시름 놓을 수 있습니다. 두 번째로, 그들은 깨끗합니다. 만약 고양이가 자거나, 놀지 않고 있다면, 대부분 자신들의 털을 핥거나, 몸을 깨끗하게 하는 중일 것입니다. 또한 그들은 자신들이 스스로 씻기 때문에 목욕이 필요 없습니다. 세 번째로, 고양이들은 매우 조용합니다. 그들은 짖지는 않지만, 가르랑거리는데, 조용하게 합니다. 게다가, 그들은 당신이 휴식을 취할 수 있게 도와줍니다. 나쁘지 않은 일이죠.

Task 3

Answers:

I have several hobbies. First, I absolutely love reading. I love fiction and poetry and can spend countless hours with my head in a book. Second, I love swimming. Whether taking a plunge in the local pool or catching some waves down by the beach, I can't imagine a better way to spend a hot summer's day. Third, I am an avid cyclist. I can never get tired of riding my bike. Be it short distance or long distance, I love to just cruise, let go of my thoughts, and be in the moment.

Translation:

나는 몇 가지의 취미를 가지고 있습니다. 첫 번째로, 나는 책 읽는 것을 굉장히 좋아합니다. 나는 소설과 시를 좋아하고 그리고 책을 읽으면서는 셀 수 없는 시간을 보낼 수도 있습니다. 두 번째로, 나는 수영을 좋아합니다. 지역 수영장에서 헤엄치기나 바다에서 파도타기든 나는 무더운 여름날을 보내기에 더 좋은 방법을 생각할 수 없습니다. 세 번째로, 나는 아주 열심인 사이클리스트 입니다. 나는 절대 자전거 타면서 지치지 않습니다. 그것이 짧은 거리든, 긴 거리든, 나는 꾸준한 속도로 달리며 생각을 흘려 보내고, 그 순간에 있는 것을 좋아합니다.

Task 4

Answers:

(1) terribly
(2) hard / well / passionately / wonderfully
(3) passionate
(4) wonderfully / well
(5) good, well

Translation:

(1) 새로운 코미디가 훌륭한 평을 받았지만, 나는 그것이 끔찍할 정도로 지루하다고 생각했습니다.
(2) 성공하고 싶다면, 당신은 열심히 일해야만 합니다.
(3) 나는 그녀가 하고 있는 모든 일과 관련해 얼마나 열정적인가에 대해 깊은 인상을 받았습니다.
(4) 그의 새로운 그림은 아주 훌륭하게 잘 나왔습니다. 색과 질감이 놀랍습니다.
(5) 나는 영어는 정말 잘하지만, 수학은 잘 하지 못합니다.

Task 5

Answers:

1. (2) 2. (1) 3. (2) 4. a 5. a

Translation:

1. 다음 중 어느 것이 주제문인가요?
   (1). 여름에 당신은 해변가에 갈 수 있습니다.
   (2) 한국에는 모두가 이용할 수 있는 많은 야외활동이 있습니다.
   (3) 겨울에 당신은 스키를 탈 수 있습니다.
   (4) 가을에 당신은 단풍을 보러 하이킹을 갈 수 있습니다.

2. 이 문장을 보세요.
   좋은 선생님은 항상 그들의 학생의 말에 귀를 기울인다.

   주제는 무엇입니까?
   (1) 좋은 선생님
   (2) 학생들

3. 이 문장을 보세요.
   예술적 재능과 수학적인 능력은 좋은 건축가의 두 가지 자격요건 입니다.

   통제하는 아이디어는 무엇인가요?
   (1). 좋은 건축가
   (2) 예술적 재능과 수학적 능력

4. 주제 문은 독자들에게 그들이 무엇을 읽을 것인지를 말해줍니다.
   a. 참
   b. 거짓

5. 중심 아이디어는 독자들에게 그 문단이 주제에 관해 논의하고자 하는 내용을 말해줍니다.
   a. 참
   b. 거짓

Task 6

Answers:

1. It also matches my laptop.
2. It's cool to hang out with friends.
3. The village also grows lots of vegetables.

Translation:

1.

나의 부모님은 정말 오래 전에 내가 고등학교를 졸업할 때 나에게 Canon AE-1 카메라를 주셨었다. 나는 그것을 카메라 가게에 가지고 가서 청소도 하고 점검을 받으려 생각하고 있습니다. 그것은 또한 내 노트북과도 잘 어울립니다. 크기도 좋지만, 대략 1995년 이후로 그것을 만진 적이 없습니다. 여전히 일반 가게에서 필름을 구입할 수 있나요? 필름이 여전히 생산되고 있나요? 몇 가지 이유로, 나는 그 오래된 옛날 카메라를 다시 사용하고 싶습니다.

2.

주말에 나는 내 Twitter 와 Facebook 페이지에 대한 작업을 하고 싶습니다. 친구들과 어울려 시간을 보내는 것은 좋습니다. 특히 Facebook은 방치되어 왔습니다. 그래서 나는 좀 Facebook 페이지를 단장하고 싶고 (weed-whacking 잡초 뽑기 / raking 갈퀴질 = 깔끔하게 정리한다는 의미) 순서대로 정리하고 싶습니다. Twitter도요. 나는 둘 다 좋긴 하지만, 지금은 그렇지 않은 시기를 겪고 있습니다. 나는 좀 더 일관성이 있는 사람이 되고 싶습니다.

3.

내가 가장 좋아하는 한국영화는 '웰컴투 동막골' 입니다. 만약 내가 외국인 친구가 있다면, 나는 이 영화를 추천할 것입니다. 이 영화는 한국 역사를 다루고, 분단의 슬픔과 이데올로기를 뛰어넘은 사랑과 우정을 그리고 있습니다. 영화의 배경은 한국전쟁의 끝쯤 입니다. 몇몇의 남한 군과 북한군이 전쟁 중 동막골에서 만나게 됩니다. 동막골은 원시림과 같이 훼손되지 않은 지역입니다. 남한과 북한은 다른 이데올로기를 가지고 있습니다. 그러나 그들은 이 영화에서 한 가지를 공유하고 있습니다. 그것은 바로 그 마을을 지키기 위해서 였습니다. 그 마을은 또한 많은 채소를 기릅니다.

Task 7

Answers:

(1) She licked the stamp, stuck it on the envelope, and dropped the letter in the box.

(2) The new manager is quite young, but he has more experience than the old manager.

(3) My new phone has a beautiful display and great apps, so I love it.

(4) I will finish this job, and after it's done I will call you.

Translation:

(1) 그녀는 우표에 침을 바르고 봉투 위에 그것을 붙였습니다. 그리고 우체통에 넣었습니다.

(2) 그 매니저는 꽤 젊지만, 그는 예전 매니저보다 더 많은 경험을 가지고 있습니다.

(3) 나의 새로운 핸드폰은 예쁜 디스플레이를 가지고 있고, 훌륭한 응용프로그램을 가지고 있습니다. 그래서 나는 그것을 정말 좋아합니다.

(4) 나는 이 일을 끝낼 것입니다. 그리고 그것이 완료된 후에 나는 당신에게 전화를 할 것입니다.

Task 8

Answers:

Cats and dogs both make great pets, and they provide joy to many families. However, they don't get along well, so if you want a pet you must choose one or the other. Since the animal might live with your family for several years, it is important to make your choice wisely. Some people enjoy winning the affection of a cat, while others prefer the steady loyalty of a dog. You can get advice about pets from friends and classmates if you need it, but ultimately the choice is yours to make.

Translation:

고양이와 개들은 둘 다 좋은 애완동물입니다. 그리고 그들은 많은 가족들에게 기쁨을 제공합니다. 그러나, 그들은 서로 잘 지내지 못합니다. 그래서 만약 당신이 애완동물을 원한다면 당신은 반드시 개 또는 고양이 중에 하나를 선택해야만 합니다. 그 동물이 당신의 가족과 몇 년간을 같이 살 것이기 때문에, 당신이 현명한 선택을 하는 것이 중요합니다. 어떤 사람들은 고양이들의 애정을 얻는 것을 즐기는 반면, 다른 사람들은 개의 지속적인 충성심을 선호합니다. 만약 필요하다면, 당신은 친구들이나 학급 친구로부터 애완동물에 대한 조언을 얻을 수 있습니다. 그렇지만, 궁극적으로 선택은 당신이 하는 것입니다.

Task 9

Answers:

(1) as soon as
(2) keep in touch
(3) psyched
(4) not an option
(5) Speaking of

Translation:

(1) 서두르세요! 우리는 당신이 숙제를 끝내자마자 떠날 수 있습니다.
(2) 나는 내 모든 친구들과 연락하려고 노력했지만, 시간을 내기가 어렵습니다.
(3) 모든 사람들은 그 여행에 대해 들 뜬 상태입니다 나는 정말로 그것이 취소되지 않았으면 좋겠습니다.
(4) 이번에, 실패는 선택이 아닙니다. 만약 당신이 그 일을 제대로 하지 않는다면, 당신은 해고 입니다.
(5) 생일 얘기 하니까 생각이 났는데, 당신의 생일이 다음달이지 않나요?

Task 10

Sample answers:

Title: The Advantages of Living in Korea

Topic: Nowadays, living in Korea has become an enjoyable experience.

Reason A: The capital Seoul has become a cosmopolitan city.

Example 1: Seoul offers all the comforts of modern life including technology.

Example 2: Also, the culture in Seoul is very diverse and there are many arts and events that reflect this diversity.

Reason B: It is easy to travel, wherever you are in Korea.

Example 1: In every city there are buses and subways that connect you to just about every corner of the map.

Example 2: You can also enjoy a trip on the KTX that will take you to any of the major cities in Korea

Concluding Sentence: Korea is truly a wonderful place to live.

Translation:

제목: 한국에서 사는 데 있어 좋은 점

주제: 요즘, 한국에서 사는 것이 즐거운 경험이 되었습니다.

이유 A: 서울, 수도는 세계적인 도시가 되었습니다.

예시1: 서울은 기술을 포함하여 현대적인 삶의 모든 편안함을 제공합니다.

예시2: 또한, 서울에서의 문화는 매우 다양하고 이러한 다양함을 반영하는 예술품과 행사들이 많습니다.

이유 B: 한국의 어디에 있든지 간에 여행하는 것은 쉽습니다.

예시 1: 지도상에 있는 모든 지역으로 연결 시켜주는 버스와 지하철이 있습니다.

예시 2: 당신은 한국 전역에 있는 모든 주요 도시들로 연결되는 KTX를 타는 여행을 즐길 수도 있습니다.

결론: 한국은 정말 살기에 멋진 곳입니다.

Task 11

Sample answers:

Reason A: Cities offer the best jobs.

Example 1: There are more jobs in the city, which offer competitive wages and stimulation.

Example 2: the most successful companies are centered in the cities.

Reason B: There are more opportunities to experience culture.

Example 1: With local art museums and city sponsored events, one can enjoy music, art and people.

Example 2: Cities also have professional sports teams and huge stadiums, which allow the public to enjoy athletic culture.

Concluding Sentence: For these reasons, city living is much more enjoyable than the countryside.

Translation:

이유 A: 도시에는 최상의 일자리들이 있습니다.

예시 1: 도시에는 경쟁력 있는 임금과 자극을 제공하는 더 많은 일거리들이 있다.

예시 2: 대부분의 성공적인 기업들은 도시에 있습니다.

이유 B: 문화를 경험할 기회가 더 많이 있습니다.

예시 1: 지역 미술관과 도시후원 행사들에서 음악, 미술, 그리고 사람들을 즐길 수 있다.

예시 2: 도시에는 또한 프로 스포츠팀과 거대한 경기장이 있는데, 그곳에서 사람들은 운동 문화를 즐길 수 있습니다.

결론: 이런 이유들에서, 도시가 시골보다 훨씬 더 살기에 즐겁다.

Task 12

Answers:

(1) such as
(2) the first is / Second
(3) For example
(4) First of all / The second

Translation:

(1) 우리는 “World English”나 “Dynamic Assessment.”와 같은 다양한 범위의 흥미로운 코스를 제공합니다.
(2) 한국드라마가 매우 인기 있는 이유에는 여러 가지가 있습니다. 첫 번째로 이야기 구조가 매우 흥미롭고 중독성이 있습니다. 두 번째, 배우들이 무척이나 매력적이고 아름답습니다.
(3) 푸에르토 리코에서는 맛있고 이국적인 과일들을 볼 수 있습니다. 예를 들어, 망고는 섬 도처에 있는 나무에서 자연상태로 자랍니다.
(4) 우리의 새 진공청소기가 시장에서 가장 좋은 제품인 까닭에는 두 가지 이유가 있습니다. 우선 첫 번째로, 매우 작고 간편합니다. 두 번째 이유는 다른 어떤 모델들보다 강력한 흡입력을 가지고 있습니다.

Task 13

Answers:

1. IC 2. DC 3. IC 4. IC 5. DC

Translation:

1. 나는 공원 주변을 산책했습니다.
2. 내가 집에 가기 전에
3. 조깅은 내 몸을 깨우고 마음을 깨끗이 해 줍니다.
5. 재미있기 때문입니다.

Task 14

Answers:

1. before　　2. after　　3. while
4. although　　5. if

Translation:

1. 당신의 의견을 덧붙이기 전에 그 사람이 말하는 것을 끝낼 때까지 기다리세요.
2. 이 미팅을 끝낸 후 나는 집에 갈 것 입니다.
3. 내가 샤워를 하는 동안 내 친구가 나에게 전화를 했었습니다.
4. 우리 엄마는 오랫동안 요리를 해왔음에도 불구하고 요리하는 것을 즐기지 않습니다.
5. 내가 선택한 대학에 가게 된다면 나는 정말 기쁠 것 입니다.

Task 15

Answers:

(1) (complex) Since the weather was so strange, we weren't able to grow enough fruit.
(2) (simple) We managed to cover the museum, the park, and the shopping district all in one day.
(3) (complex) He only smokes while he is drinking with his buddies from home.
(4) (compound) My wife likes to read, while I prefer watching television.

Translation:

예: 이 시험에서의 성공은 내게 많은 의미를 지니기 때문에 나는 잘할 결심을 했습니다.

(1) 날씨가 너무 이상했기 때문에, 우리는 과일들을 충분히 기를 수 없었습니다.
(2) 우리는 박물관, 공원, 쇼핑거리를 하루에 돌아보기로 계획을 세웠습니다.
(3) 그는 그의 고향친구들과 술을 마시는 동안에만 담배를 피웁니다.
(4) 내가 텔레비전 보는 것을 선호하는 반면에, 내 아내는 읽기를 좋아합니다.

Task 16

Sample answers:

(1) When he calls you tonight, don't answer the phone.
(2) Since I love you so much, I will give you a discount.
(3) Last night after we met, I completely forgot your name.
(4) (no change)
(5) Because you never listen, I am going to let you do the talking.

Translation:

(1) 오늘 밤에 그가 당신에게 전화를 걸었을 때, 응답하지 마세요.
(2) 당신을 너무 사랑하기 때문에, 할인을 해 드리겠습니다.
(3) 어제 저녁 우리가 만난 후, 나는 당신의 이름을 완전히 잊어버렸습니다.
(4) 그녀가 어디를 가든 그녀는 행복합니다.
(5) 당신은 절대 듣지 않기 때문에, 나는 당신에게 말하는 것을 하게 할 것입니다.

Task 17

Answers:

(1) deprived
(2) impressed / impressive
(3) get it
(4) hit the books
(5) well-rounded

Translation:

(1) Jake는 현재 매우 열심히 공부합니다. 왜냐하면 어린 시절 교육을 충분히 받지 못했기 때문입니다.
(2) 우리는 처음과 끝 부분이 매우 인상 깊었습니다. 하지만 중간은 그렇게 인상적이지 않았습니다.
(3) 그녀는 나에게 지시를 설명하려 시도했습니다. 하지만 저는 알아듣지 못했습니다.
(4) 큰 시험 전에 열심히 공부하는 것은 중요합니다. 하지만 숙면을 취하는 것 또한 중요합니다.
(5) 모든 사람들은 이 학교의 학생들이 가장 균형 잡혔다고 말합니다. 하지만 제게는 학생들이 남들과 같은 활동, 기술 그리고 흥미를 가지고 있는 것처럼 보입니다.

Task 18

Sample answers:

1. In my view, plastic surgery is harmful to our society
2. I believe that walking is really good for your health.
3. In my opinion, pasta tastes best with red wine.
4. I think that the first singer was much better than the second.
5. According to the professor, the exam should not be too difficult.

Translation:

1. 내 관점으로는, 성형수술은 우리사회에 해가 됩니다.
2. 저는 걷는 것이 건강에 좋다고 믿습니다.
3. 제 의견으로는 파스타는 레드와인과 가장 잘 어울린다고 생각합니다.
4. 제 생각에 첫 번째 가수가 두 번째 가수보다 훨씬 잘했습니다.
5. 교수님에 따르면, 시험이 그렇게 어렵지는 않을 것입니다.

Task 19

Sample answers:

1. Topic: Plastic Surgery.
   Opinion: In my opinion, plastic surgery is harmful to our society.
   Support: There are risks in surgery and the results can be fatal. (fact)
   Support: Society should be more accepting of different types of beauty and not pressure people to all look the same. (opinion)

2. Topic: Hagwons in Korea.
   Opinion: In my opinion, Hagwons are very poor places for students to learn.
   Support: Many operate at night, taking away from the child's rest time. (fact)
   Support: It seems that students at Hagwons tend to spend more time socializing with friends than actually studying. (opinion)

3. Topic: Blind Dates
   Opinion: In my opinion, blind dates should be avoided.
   Support: Going on a date with a person whom you've never met could be awkward. (fact)
   Support: It's better to date someone having at least met them, so you know that you share some interest. (opinion)

Translation:

1. 주제: 성형 수술
   의견: 내 의견으로는, 성형 수술은 우리 사회에 해를 준다.
   뒷받침: 수술에는 위험이 따르고 결과는 치명적일 수 있다. (사실)
   뒷받침: 사회는 다양한 타입의 아름다움을 더 받아들여야 하며 사람들이 다 똑같이 생기기를 강요해서는 안 된다. (의견)

2. 주제: 한국의 학원들
   의견: 내 의견으로는, 학원은 좋지 않은 학습 방법이다.

뒷받침: 대부분의 학원은 밤에 운영되며, 어린이들이 쉴 시간을 빼앗는다. (사실)
뒷받침: 학생들이 학원에서 공부를 하기 보다는 친구들과 어울리는 경향이 더 강한 것으로 보인다. (의견)

3. 주제: 블라인드 데이트
의견: 내 의견으로는, 블라인드 데이트는 피해야 한다.
뒷받침: 한 번도 만나본 적이 없는 사람과 데이트를 하는 것은 어색할 수 있다. (사실)
뒷받침: 적어도 한 번은 만난 적이 있어서 공유하는 관심사가 있는 사람과 데이트하는 것이 더 낫다. (의견)

Task 20

Answers:

(1) In the event of trouble please contact the Help Desk, which is located in the Administrative Office.
(2) I fell in love with one of my coworkers, which really confused my parents.
(3) The decision will be made by the committee, which is a group of people elected by the shareholders.
(4) You should think carefully about choosing your advisor, who is the one that will help you the most.
(5) The referee from last night's game, who made several bad calls, was attacked this morning.

Translation:

(1) 문제가 발생하면 행정 실에 위치한 헬프데스크에 연락해주세요.
(2) 나는 내 동료 중 한 명과 사랑에 빠졌는데, 그것은 내 부모님을 무척이나 혼란스럽게 했습니다.
(3) 주주들에 의해 선출된 사람들의 모임인 위원회에서 결정은 내려질 것입니다.
(4) 당신은 조언자를 고르는 것을 신중하게 생각해야 하는데, 그는 당신을 가장 많이 도와줄 사람입니다.
(5) 어젯밤 게임의 심판은 몇 번의 오심을 했었는데, 오늘 아침에 공격을 당했습니다.

STEP BY STEP **영작문**

초판 1쇄 발행　2013년 4월 10일
초판 2쇄 발행　2019년 2월 27일

지은이	성은경
발행인	김인철
총괄 · 기획	가정준 Director, University Knowledge Press
편집장	신선호 Executive Knowledge Contents Creator
도서편집	박현정 Contents Creator
전자책편집	인은주 e-Contents Creator
재무관리	강현주 Managing Creator
사전 · 출판	정준희 Contents Creator
마케팅 파트장	백승이 Chief Marketing Creator
마케팅	이현진 Marketing Creator
발행처	한국외국어대학교 지식출판콘텐츠원 02450 서울특별시 동대문구 이문로 107 전화 02)2173-2493~7 FAX 02)2173-3363 홈페이지 http://press.hufs.ac.kr 전자우편 press@hufs.ac.kr 출판등록 제6-6호(1969. 4. 30)
디자인 · 편집	디자인퍼브 02)2254-4308
인쇄 · 제본	네오프린텍 02)718-3111

ISBN 978-89-7464-830-5　13740　　정가 14,000원

* 잘못된 책은 교환하여 드립니다.

HU:NE 은 한국외국어대학교 지식출판콘텐츠원의 어학도서, 사회과학도서, 지역학 도서 Sub Brand이다. 한국외대의 영문명인 HUFS, 현명한 국제전문가 양성(International+Intelligent)의 의미를 담고 있으며, 휴인(携引)의 뜻인 '이끌다, 끌고 나가다'라는 의미처럼 출판계를 이끄는 리더로서, 혁신의 이미지를 담고 있다.